How To Produce A Fashion Show

How To Produce A Fashion Show

Mary Ellen Diehl

Fairchild Publications, New York

To Frances and Altman Diehl

Copyright © 1976, by Fairchild Publications
Division of Capital Cities Media, Inc.
Third Printing 1981

All rights reserved. No part of this book may be reproduced in any form without permission in writing from the publisher, except by a reviewer who wishes to quote sources in connection with a review written for inclusion in a magazine or newspaper.

Standard Book Number: 87005-159-8

Library of Congress Catalog Card Number: 76-20221

Printed in the United States of America

Acknowledgments

The author wishes to acknowledge with thanks the special help of the late Katherine Murphy, Vice President and Fashion Director, Bloomingdale's, Barbara Scholey, Book Designer and Olga Kontzias, Editor, Fairchild Publications, Inc.

Thanks also to the following people for their contributions: Marcia Anderson, Videotape Program Director, Saks Fifth Avenue; Eleanor Becker, Executive Editor, *Bride's;* Lenore Benson, Merchandising Director, *Mademoiselle;* Joanne Black, Advertising Manager, Celanese Fibers Marketing Co.; Marsha Breen, Publicity Director, Saks Fifth Avenue; Michael Collins; Rose Conroy, Merchandising Director, *Redbook;* Claire E. Devener, Public Relations, Air France; Barbara Doljack, Merchandising Director, *Seventeen;* Iiean Helland, Director of Retail Programs, *Modern Bride;* Gloria King, Gloria King Associates; Susan Loren, Account Executive, Ogilvy & Mather; Gillis MacGil, Director, Mannequin Fashion Models Agency, Inc.; Barrett McKee, General Manager, Retail Sales, CBS Television Stations, New York; Barbara McKibbin, Marketing Director, *Vogue;* Eleanor McMillen, Executive Director, The Fashion Group, Inc.; Sylvia Mohr; National Foundation of the March of Dimes; Pat Nilson, Marketing Relations Director, Simplicity Pattern Co.; Linnéa Person, Merchandising Services Editor, *Vogue;* June B. Roche, Corporate Fashion Director, Deering Milliken, Inc.; Irene Ruperti; Irene Satz, Fashion Director, Ohrbach's; Doris Shaw, Advertising Director, Saks Fifth Avenue; Larry Sherman, Steve Sohmer, Inc.; Steve Sohmer, Steve Sohmer, Inc.; Pat Thavenot, Merchandising Director, *Glamour;* John Terrell, Public Relations Director, Sears, Roebuck & Co.; Merle Thomason, Costume Librarian, Fairchild Publications, Inc.; Bobbi Van; Ed Witkowski, Periodicals Librarian, Fashion Institute of Technology.

Contents

1 History of the Fashion Show — 1
2 Why Have A Fashion Show? — 13
3 Types of Fashion Shows — 21
4 Background and Advance Planning — 27
5 Planning the Merchandise: Garments and Accessories — 41
6 The Fitting, Run-Off and Rehearsal — 49
7 Models—Choosing, Training and Evaluating Them — 59
8 Commentator and Commentary — 71
9 Setting Up For The Show: The Floor Plan — 83
10 Store Sponsored Promotion — 91
11 Promotional Tie-Ins and Giveaways — 99
12 Advertising and Publicity — 109
13 Shows Requiring Special Handling — 117
14 Film, Tape and Television Presentations — 137
Bibliography — 145
Index — 147

History of the Fashion Show | 1

The fashion show as we know it is the child of American ready-to-wear. The idea of dressing models and parading them down a runway was born out of the mid-western apparel marts, during the early days of mass production. The innovator is unknown but most probably the fashion show originated in Chicago around 1911. However, the idea of showing current fashion on *inanimate* forms dates back to the 14th century.

Model, or fashion, dolls were the first means of circulating the latest styles of dress with any accuracy. The word *"doll"* was not commonly used until about 1750—it had not even appeared in a dictionary until 1700. Prior to that, model dolls were referred to as puppets, dummies, poupées, courriers and later on in the United States as "little ladies" or "fashion babies."

Both Paris and Venice lay claim to the first of these dolls—life-size forms dressed to show the latest fashions. Since Venice was in its zenith as the Queen of the Adriatic, it seems probable that the dolls first appeared there at the annual fair on Assumption Day in the early part of the 14th century. They were displayed in the styles that would be fashionable during the coming year.

Later, it became the practice of the Hotel Rambouillet in Paris to display two life-size dolls dressed in the current fashions. *"La grande Pandora"* was fitted out from head to toe each time the fashions changed. The smaller of the dolls, *"la petite Pandora,"* wore the appropriate underclothes.

Their status was confirmed in 1391 when Charles VI of France sent dolls to the Queen of England in the court dress introduced by Queen Isabella of Bavaria. These dolls were full-sized, the clothes made to the English Queen's measurements—presumably, they were wearable as well as reproduceable.

In 1496, Queen Anne of Britanny ordered a large doll to be sent to the Spanish Queen Isabella. And in 1600, just prior to their marriage, Henry IV of France wrote Maria de Medici, "Frontenac tells me you desire patterns of our fashions

Model Dolls

Early 19th century French fashion doll in Russian Court Dress. (Warwick Doll Museum. Copyright, Walter Scott, Bradford, England.)

1

HOW TO PRODUCE A FASHION SHOW

in dress. I send you therefore some model dolls."

Fashion dolls hit their stride in the 17th and 18th centuries. Dolls were sent to all parts of Europe and as far away as Russia by milliners, dressmakers and hairdressers. (In 1763, the great hairdresser, Legros, exhibited thirty dolls showing creations. A few years later, a hundred dolls were used to show the latest hair fashions.) The dolls illustrated current styles in jewelry (often real) as well as hair and dress styles. When a number of small courts sprang up creating a heavier demand for appropriate wardrobes and greater interest in the dolls as a means of keeping up with the current fashions, it became the mode for fashionable ladies to keep a pair of dolls, similar to the two "pandoras," for outer- and underwear. As Paris gained fashion ascendancy, the European capitals became so dependent on the flow of dolls from there for the fashion news that when France and England were at war, a four-foot high alabaster model doll, "le grand courrier de la mode," was allowed through the closed ports by mutual consent.

Rose Bertin, the best known dressmaker of her day, used the dolls as advertisements for her services. She outfitted Marie Antoinette and her model dolls in her creations.

The French Revolution contributed indirectly to the art of dressing the dolls. Many of the disenfranchised aristocrats fled to London where their talents for fine embroidery went into the making of clothes for the dolls.

The dolls began appearing in America during the early 18th century. They were relied on to keep the country current with London and Paris. Travelers were urged to send back dolls from Europe. Because of the long trip, many were smaller than life-size—some about twelve-inches high, wearing gold and silver jewelry set with precious stones. A newspaper ad from 1733 indicated how prized they were:

> "To be seen at Mrs. Hannah Teatts, mantuamaker, at the head of Summer Street, Boston, a baby dressed after the newest fashions of mantuas and nightgowns and everything belonging to a dress, lately arrived on the 'Captain White' from London."

Until 1850, the dolls were most often executed in wax, wood or cloth. After 1850 paper-mâché was used, allowing for more detail in head styles. Their popularity lasted well into the 19th century when their importance was gradually superseded by the French fashion plates and later, fashion magazines.

Vogue Magazine's Model Doll Show

By the end of the 19th century the dolls had become novelties rather than a viable means of keeping current with fashions.

After a successful model doll show in London, *Vogue,* then not quite four years old, staged its first "Model Doll Show" in New York in 1896. It was an exhibit rather than a fashion show, but notable for several reasons. The show was a charity event, sponsored by some of the most prominent society women of the day, with the proceeds benefiting a local hospital. It was undoubtedly one of the first times a fashion presentation had been used as a fund-raising event.

HISTORY OF THE FASHION SHOW

Model Doll Show

UNDER THE MANAGEMENT OF VOGUE

IN AID OF

THE SCARLET FEVER AND DIPHTHERIA HOSPITAL

SHERRY'S, MARCH 20TH, 21ST AND 23D

THE Show will be opened with a Private View, Friday, 20 March, at 3 o'clock, and continue on Saturday, 21 March, and Monday 23 March. The extraordinary feature will be dolls dressed as models of special costumes and of prevailing fashions. These dolls will be dressed by the leading designers of New York, and present a great variety of subject and treatment.

TICKETS — — — FIFTY CENTS

PATRONESSES:

Mrs. Charles B. Alexander	Mrs. Richard H. Derby	Mrs. Eugene Kelly	Mrs. C. Albert Stevens
Miss Malvina Appleton	Mrs. Arthur M. Dodge	Mrs. Edward King	Mrs. William Rhinelander
Mrs. John Jacob Astor	Mrs. Cleveland H. Dodge	Mrs. Gustav Kissel	Mrs. Joseph Stickney
Mrs. Charles T. Barney	Mrs. John R. Drexel	Mrs. Luther Kountze	Mrs. T. Suffern Tailer
Miss de Barril	Mrs. Nicholas Fish	Mrs. Charles Lanier	Mrs. Henry A. C. Taylor
Mrs. Edmund L. Baylies	Miss de Forest	Mrs. J. Lawrence Lee	Mrs. Jonathan Thorne
Mrs. August Belmont	Mrs. George B. de Forest	Mrs. Edward A. Le Roy, Jr.	Mrs. Henry Graff Trevor
Mrs. David Wolfe Bishop	Miss Furniss	Mrs. Charles H. Marshall	Mrs. John B. Trevor
Mrs. Heber R. Bishop	Mrs. John Lyon Gardiner	Mrs. Ogden Mills	Mrs. Paul Tuckerman
Mrs. William T. Blodgett	Mrs. Elbridge T. Gerry	Mrs. John W. Minturn	Mrs. Arthur Turnure
Mrs. James A. Burden	Mrs. G. G. Haven	Mrs. Trenor L. Park	Mrs. Cornelius Vanderbilt
Miss Callender	Mrs. Peter Cooper Hewitt	Mrs. James W. Pinchot	Mrs. F. W. Vanderbilt
Mrs. A. Cass Canfield	Mrs. Thomas Hitchcock	Mrs. George B. Post	Mrs. William Seward Webb
Mrs. Henry E. Coe	Mrs. G. G. Howland	Mrs. M. Taylor Pyne	Mrs. Geo. Peabody Wetmore
Mrs. Joseph H. Choate	Mrs. Edward W. Humphreys	Mrs. Jules Reynal	Mrs. John C. Wilmerding
Mrs. H. H. Curtis	Mrs. Morris K. Jesup	Mrs. T. J. Oakley Rhinelander	Mrs. Orme Wilson
Mrs. Brockholst Cutting	Mrs. William Jay	Mrs. Sidney Dillon Ripley	Mrs. Buchanan Winthrop
Miss Cuyler	Mrs. Walter Jennings	Mrs. Henry Sloane	Mrs. Frank Spencer Withers
Mrs. Francis Delafield	Mrs. Frederic R. Jones	Mrs. William Douglas Sloane	

Further particulars, if desired, will be supplied by the management,
VOGUE, 154 FIFTH AVENUE, NEW YORK.

This invitation in 1896 drew over 1,000 people. Vogue's assessment: "It has benefitted the Scarlet Fever and Diphtheria Hospital; it has benefitted the American dressmaker; it has benefitted Vogue itself, and it has created a new form of entertainment, which has the supreme merit of being founded on utility." (Copyright, 1896, by The Fashion Company. Courtesy of Vogue Magazine, The Condé Nast Publications Inc.)

In addition, the one hundred and fifty miniature dolls displayed "... wonderful variety of color and costume, and carried out much more effectively than the most sanguine wishes had pictured the original idea, as conceived by *Vogue*, of a worthy expression of dress by leading American dressmakers." The promotion of America's designers over those of London and Paris, which peaked around both world wars and again in the Sixties, made its first appearance at this model doll show.

3

HOW TO PRODUCE A FASHION SHOW

Two of the earliest fashion show "co-commentators" from Vogue Magazine's 1914 "Fashion Fête."

HISTORY OF THE FASHION SHOW

The French Contribution

The fashion show owes a great deal of its development to the inventiveness of Charles Frederick Worth and the showmanship of Paul Poiret.

The courts of Louis XIV and Louis XV had made elegance and France synonymous. Worth, an Englishman, is responsible for turning the French couture into very nearly what it is today. In 1845, when Worth arrived in Paris, there was no couture to speak of. There had been well-known French dressmakers, Rose Bertin being one, but they were just that, *dressmakers* not *designers*. A woman selected a pattern, originally from a fashion doll, and by 1850, from a fashion plate appearing in one of the numerous publications of the time. She would next select fabric and trimmings; and her final stop was the dressmaker's, where the garment was made up according to specifications. A firm such as Gagelin & Opigez, where Worth worked, was noted for its fabric and trimmings and a few ready-made items such as shawls and cloaks. It's not clear when the practice of showing items on a live "model" developed, but in Worth's time it was part of the job of the *demoiselle de magazin* (shopgirl). (Marie Vernet, his future wife, worked at Gagelin & Opigez in this capacity.) When Worth opened his own firm in 1858, he not only revolutionized the couture by designing for an individual woman's type and personality, but he used his wife to model his creations in his maison. As Worth became more successful, he employed a number of mannequins to show his collections to customers—the word "mannequin" was coined by a newspaper reporter in an article on the House of Worth. Later, Worth would give a new idea exposure by persuading one of his prominent patrons to wear it to an event, and within days, orders for it would start to come in (a practice used by Rose Bertin as well).

The Paris fashions of Worth's early days were more serviceable than chic or imaginative. Worth, under the patronage of the Second Empire, brought back the opulent, luxurious fabrics and heavy trims of earlier periods of French dress. Even after he became established as the leading couturier and dressmaker to the Empress Eugénie, women still patronized couturiers only for special gowns—court dresses, ball gowns, costumes for masked balls. Whether Worth invented the hated crinoline, or the Empress Eugénie did to hide her thickening figure, he is identified with overly elaborate gowns, laden with trim and a heavily corseted silhouette which must have been agony to endure. Nevertheless, he gave Paris *couture* and in the process gave the fashion industry live models.

While Worth created the modern couture, Paul Poiret, a Frenchman, extended its range. He radically changed the feminine silhouette and in the process, developed techniques of fashion promotion that we continue to use.

Poiret's most lasting contribution is in the areas of art and design. In his formative years, he studied art and haunted the Comédie Française, and the museums and galleries of Paris. Perhaps his eye for line and color and his sense of the dramatic were developed during this period. In any case, Poiret felt a continuing obligation to support both the fine and decorative arts, and he became

A flare of footlights, a moment of silence, the curtains part, and—America passes judgment on what America can do

Models parade in 1914 "Fashion Fête." (Left and this page: Copyright, 1914, by The Vogue Company. Courtesy of Vogue Magazine, The Condé Nast Publications Inc.)

HOW TO PRODUCE A FASHION SHOW

Jean Patou with one of his mannequins in 1924. (KEYSTONE)

the catalyst that popularized Art Deco. He put the unknown Raoul Dufy to work designing his stationery, then his fabrics; he developed the soft-focus technique we use today in fashion photography; he engaged a struggling young painter named Edward Steichen to execute the photographs of his collections. He used Man Ray, who in the process of photographing Poiret's 1922 collection invented his Rayograph. Poiret printed and circulated, at his own expense, booklets of his current designs. The artists Poiret selected, Paul Iribe, Georges Lepape, Erté, among others, were to permanently change the art of fashion illustration. Their wonderful, exotic creations can be seen throughout the 1920's and 1930's on the covers of *Vogue* and *Harper's Bazaar*.

Poiret was born in 1879 and, using leftover scraps of silk, began "designing" on a small wooden dummy while apprenticed to an umbrella maker. He began sketching, and then selling, his fashions and was eventually hired by Doucet in 1898. Doucet was considered one of the best dressed men of the day; Poiret adopted his style of dress and his elegance. Despite Poiret's success, he was fired from Doucet's for offending a client and after a brief stint designing for the House of Worth, opened his own shop in 1903.

Poiret's flair surfaced first with his window displays—they depicted the Isle de France and changed with the seasons. The window displays caused more comment than patronage—but Poiret was firmly launched when he began designing for Réjane and other highly visible members of Paris society. From then on his personal stamp could be seen on everything he turned his hand to.

In contrast to Worth's opulence, Poiret developed an intimate and sensual look to his clothes. His fabrics were soft; his colors more vivid. He was the first couturier to design casual "sports" clothes.

He introduced an Oriental feeling to some of his clothes, daringly slit tunics and skirts to show boots underneath. In 1910, he designed the hobble skirt, tapered at the bottom to restrict movement to little mincing steps. However, Poiret more than made up for this whim by launching a more natural, feminine figure controlled with a girdle-like garment he designed himself—releasing women from six hundred years of tight corseting.

Poiret used his promotional instincts to generate free publicity. He toured chic resorts, Russia and various other countries making personal appearances and giving fashion showings which were tremendous successes. He was among the first couturiers to parade his mannequins at the races—showing pieces from his latest collection to great effect. A less successful effort was his attempted conquest of the United States in 1913. Poiret recognized the potential of the American market, but his critical comments were widely reported. Throughout his career, he entertained on a lavish scale, throwing huge parties, theatrical presentations and costume balls. They were colorful extravaganzas, well covered in the press. After World War I, he was still a byword among fashionable women, but he never recaptured the momentum or the timeliness of his pre-war years.

HISTORY OF THE FASHION SHOW

The House of Paquin made several contributions to the fashion show. The tenor was more conservative than Poiret, but Paquin began the practice of showing at big social gatherings. He paraded his models at the racetrack and at the opening night of the opera. Paquin also began staging a tableau as the finale to his openings—in one show he presented twenty mannequins in white evening dresses.

Patou also had an impact on the fashion show in several areas. He introduced gala evenings which were aimed at Paris society and even more strongly at the press. After his first trip to the United States, Patou returned with six American models who caused a great stir and established the American figure, more athletic than that of the European woman, as the fashionable ideal.

By the early 1900's, the use of live models to show fashions was well established for private customers and the press, both inside the couture houses and outside, at special galas and social events.

But it took the American clothing manufacturers who "showed" at the major regional apparel marts and the impetus of the growing ready-to-wear business to put models on a runway and organize them into a fashion show. Although the first ready-made dresses were known as early as 1904, the industry did not take hold strongly until about 1915–16, when mass production techniques were refined. By 1908 or 1909, the industry was developed enough to hold trade shows on a regular basis, the most important of which were in Chicago and New York.

In July 1910, *Women's Wear** reported:

"Popularity of Ready-Made Dresses Injuring Business of Small Dressmakers and Sales of Piece Goods."

In the same issue, the upcoming "Third Annual Wearing Apparel, Style and Fabric Show" was reported. In subsequent issues, the exhibits and "demonstrated displays" were duly noted—but no live models and no fashion shows.

By 1911 "living models" were used in the United States as a regular part of fashion promotions for retailers as well as manufacturers. However, from the reports, they seemed to be more akin to informal modeling than to a fashion parade. The runway show must have evolved rapidly from this because *Women's Wear* carried a report in its August 10, 1912 issue on the "Merchandise Buyers Exposition and Fashion Show at the New Grand Central Palace (N.Y.)." The event featured two fashion shows daily on living models, with cards on stage indicating manufacturers' names—"no lecturing." An orchestra rendered popular songs during the showing.

By 1913, most retailers were using the fashion show to introduce their season's styles. The following is a typical account from *The American Cloak and Suit Review*, May 1913:

"The Shenk Store in Lebanon, Pennsylvania Utilizes Living Models for Its Spring Opening Display.

*The word *Daily* was added in 1927.

The First Runway Show

A Shenk Store fashion show, 1913. "Timing models" quickly became an enormous drawing card.

7

> "Shenk's was among the up-to-date retailers who utilized the services of living models for the display of women's wearing apparel at their spring opening in the garment department . . . (It) served to boom spring business and bring about an increase in sales.
>
> "The show was held on three afternoons and evenings. A platform was built in the center of the garment department, and a player piano was used for the furnishing of music. Four models, two for women's garments and two for misses' garments, showed the new spring apparel in tailored suits, coats, lingerie, dresses, silk evening gowns and wraps, which ranged in price from $10 all the way up to $150."

These shows employed elaborate scenery and props to recreate the exact settings in which the merchandise would be worn. Many of them ran two and a half to three hours.

Innovations followed rapidly. John Wanamaker, the leading retailer of the day, in a showing of Poiret designs, inaugurated "a most unique and original idea, namely the simultaneous entry of a masculine and feminine model." Often when shows were put on for several days running, the merchandise changed every day, with the bridal party being used to close it on the final day. The shows were an instant success—one retailer estimated fourteen to fifteen thousand people attended a week long promotion, drawn mostly by the fashion shows.

The most spectacular of the early fashion shows was the "Chicago Fall & Winter Style Show," August 18, 1914. It was billed as the "greatest show in the world"—a three day exhibition including a "Living Model Exhibit" with two hundred and fifty garments shown before an audience of five thousand people. The show was divided into seasons and interspersed with entertainment. Each backdrop was elaborately executed and the finale included floats entitled "American Beauties" and "Goddess of Fashion." The show was filmed for distribution to retailers who would show it in their local theaters along with their own merchandise.

Whether time blurred the circumstances, or Edna Woolman Chase was out of touch with the ready-to-wear industry (not surprising, given the status of the industry—and of *Vogue*—at the time), her claim to inventing the fashion show in 1914 is at odds with reports in the trade publications. She did, however, invest the fashion show with a chic and social acceptance which it lacked.

At the beginning of World War I, the flow of news from Paris was threatened. As the new editor of *Vogue*, Chase was hard-pressed for fashion ideas to report —in fact for authoritative fashion of any kind. Remembering the success of the "Model Doll Shows" which she had been involved with in the late 1890's, and their emphasis on American designers, she decided to stage a "Fashion Fête," featuring the best of American designs. With the patronage of leading society women of the day, the show was presented on November 4, 5 and 6—the models "turned left, right and walked down the aisle (runways were a later refinement)."

HISTORY OF THE FASHION SHOW

A 1913 show by a Wisconsin retailer. The backdrop was borrowed from a Cleveland trade show held earlier in the season.

This was the first of many shows sponsored by *Vogue*, including a couture show the following year presented in the form of a play, at the designers' request.

By the 1920's, ready-to-wear departments were firmly established as a key part of the retailer's business. And with it, the fashion show. No longer a novelty, the fashion show was the accepted medium for introducing and promoting apparel.

When Neiman-Marcus opened its doors in 1907, Sanger Bros. was the leading retailer in Texas. Herbert Marcus recognized early the significance of ready-to-wear and that, plus good merchandising and promotional instincts, soon put the store in a dominant position. Among the innovations was the first weekly fashion show in the country. In the late 1920's, Stanley Marcus sponsored (and commentated) a show at a local hotel using the Ted Weems band for background music —an idea that was quickly adopted by other retailers.

Later, he produced the first "definitive" bridal show with bridal and maids gowns, whole trousseaux, lingerie and gifts, in several different price ranges. A bridal magazine editor was brought in to co-commentate.

From Novelty to Necessity

HOW TO PRODUCE A FASHION SHOW

A 1971 Fashion Group presentation. Most backdrops were designed for easy transport to regional meetings. (Courtesy of The Fashion Group.)

In the middle Thirties, the fashion show was beginning to be produced on a grand scale. It became a publicity tool, a source of entertainment—professionally executed, new techniques and applications were invented for it. The fashion show moved into new media.

It was inevitable that the fashion show would take to radio. In 1934, a noted fashion authority, Tobé, commentated a benefit from a New York hotel which was simultaneously broadcast to twelve cities around the country. It was so successful that others quickly followed.

The Chicago Century of Progress Exhibition in 1933–34 gave impetus to the popularity of the fashion show. As did movie studios which used it as a publicity vehicle for their films, magazines and newspapers around the country.

The Fashion Group, founded by and for women fashion executives in 1931, has staged some of the most creative fashion shows over the years. Their first large show, "Fashion Futures," was launched at the Hotel Astor in 1935. Geared to its members and the press, it included manufacturers, importers, designers and wholesalers as well as retailers. Since it was an informative showing of generic

HISTORY OF THE FASHION SHOW

fashions, none of the participants was credited. Taking up a recurrent theme—promoting American designers to American retailers—and ultimately their customers—the Fashion Group staged a "Fashion Futures-American Edition" in 1937; it included seven hundred dresses, hats, furs, suits—worn by one hundred and six models on two stages in twenty-two scenes. As the presentations grew more and more elaborate, the Fashion Group reported (on a 1941 show):

> "We rivaled the town's best musicals in stage sets, lighting, drama, gorgeous girls, and in cost of production, too. We spent $47,000 on that show—$13,000 for mannequins alone..."

From 1942 to 1950, *The New York Times* presented its "Fashions of The Times" in October and November of each year. Together with the Sunday supplement of the same name, it not only presented directional looks year after year, it established the fashion authority of the *Times* and brought in a steady stream of apparel and retail advertising.

From the early Forties on, Eleanor Lambert, a well-known public relations and publicity consultant, did more than anyone to *spectacularize* the fashion show. She organized higher priced manufacturers into the Couture Group, whose showings drew fashion editors from all over the country. Her Annual Coty American Fashion Critics' Awards, begun in 1943 still generates enormous publicity. The fashion shows that epitomized the extravaganzas of that time were the "March of Dimes" shows for the National Foundation. People paid one hundred dollars to watch Broadway stars, celebrities and personalities commentate, model and perform, and for the fashions, of course.

To celebrate the golden anniversary of the consolidation of the five boroughs and twenty-seven cities into Greater New York, a gala fashion show was held in the Grand Central Palace (the scene of some of the earliest trade shows). Highlights included a parade of one hundred models opening the show by descending a golden ramp in fashions contributed by the entire New York apparel market. Twenty ballet dancers performed wearing black and gold dresses—each under twenty dollars. The finale was the traditional bridal scene—in this case, five brides representing the boroughs and a Golden Jubilee Bride.

One of the last remaining examples of this type of event is the Deering Milliken Breakfast Show. Started in 1952, the Breakfast Show represents a major promotional thrust to the trade by this textile firm. Twice yearly, buyers and the press view this Broadway-style musical. Through dialogue studded with industry in-jokes, song and dance routines and skits, the audience learns about the various fibers and fabrics, which manufacturers are making what and the important styles and colors of the next season.

The first shows were stationary exhibits, then tableaux, which evolved into the fashion parades. As extravagant as they became in the Thirties, Forties and Fifties, this basic form remained unchanged.

The Fashion Show Is Re-Invented

HOW TO PRODUCE A FASHION SHOW

The spectacular Deering Milliken Breakfast Show uses a cast of Broadway singers, dancers and actors in a series of production numbers. (Courtesy of Deering Milliken Inc.)

It was inevitable that with the explosion of creativity and vitality—not to mention the fashion changes—in the Sixties, the old form would be affected.

Mary Quant's press showing to open her second London boutique effected permanent changes in this traditional format of the fashion show. Her innovations became the hallmarks of the contemporary show. Presented on photographic rather than runway models, the show was a steady stream of movement (helped with large fans) and energy—the same qualities that characterized her clothes. Models danced and whirled down a stairway and around the audience. The action was coordinated with taped music that completely replaced the commentary.

Later in the Sixties, coordinated sound and light shows were integrated into the fashion shows. Multi-media presentations were used, with the addition of both slides and movie backgrounds to give an even greater sense of action to the fashion show.

Why Have a Fashion Show? | 2

You don't need to understand soft goods merchandising in order to put on a fashion show—but it helps. As we will see, fashion shows are sponsored by different groups with different aims. The greatest majority, however, are staged by retailers and planned and executed by either the store fashion coordinator or the special events director.

Regardless of who is sponsoring the show, the time and money invested in it must produce results. Knowing the marketplace in general is a big plus in mounting a show that will produce the desired results.

In the American marketplace, you can buy all sorts of merchandise and services. Apparel and accessories are known as soft goods, as opposed to packaged goods (health and beauty aids, etc.).

How does one sell these items? Traditionally, apparel is sold via a "merchandising" approach. A fashion is created, promoted to the "trade"—the retailer who stocks it. It is touted in the fashion publications and (hopefully) appears so irresistible that the consumer goes to her favorite store and buys it. The primary thrust in soft goods is toward the trade. The retailer is critical because the consumer must be able to see, feel and try on the article for a sale to be made in the store she shops at. Conversely, the sale can not be made if the article isn't accessible to the consumer. Soft goods items are merchandised: pushed through the distribution pipeline from manufacturer to retailer to consumer.

Packaged goods, on the other hand, tend to be sold using a marketing approach. The item is promoted to the consumer so strongly that retailers must carry it to satisfy consumer demand (or risk losing the customer to a competitor). This pulls the item from the manufacturer to the consumer.

There are other differences as well. The marketing approach calls for the needs of the consumer to be identified; a product is created to satisfy the need, or an existing product is repositioned or repackaged in line with that need. Although clothing is a basic human need, fashion isn't. And to date, fashion has been the ingredient that sells apparel. Soft goods advertising to the consumer (secondary

Soft Goods Merchandising— What Is It?

to the trade thrust) has concentrated on creating desire rather than satisfying need. Also, the two approaches may have developed along different lines because while there are less than three thousand department and specialty stores in this country—outlets for apparel—there are hundreds of thousands of outlets for packaged goods—drug stores, supermarkets, hardware stores, etc.

This is a simple view of soft goods merchandising and packaged goods marketing. Both systems have worked in the past to distribute vast quantities of goods.

The Changing Marketplace

The American market as a whole is in a state of flux, and retailing with it. The cost of labor and raw materials is rapidly rising. The consumer is much more demanding than before, much more cost conscious. Furthermore, the consumer no longer buys an item simply because it's new, or that a fashion publication promotes it, or that it will make her look like someone she admires. Both women and men are more selective and more individual in their clothes-buying, and anyone hoping to sell them must be aware of this and cater to it.

Another point to consider: there are more and more goods and services on the market each year which means more competition for the dollars normally spent on clothing. And this, when the buying power of the dollar is shrinking, and family incomes are not growing as fast as they once did.

In addition, the department store (particularly) is being threatened by the expansion of chains, discount and drug stores, even supermarkets, into its regular merchandise categories.

This has a direct bearing on retailing. With the keener competition for the customer's dollar, retailers are adopting more and more principles of the marketing systems. Standard procedures include development of new markets or expansion of current ones; defining and controlling the ratio between "input"—the energy and dollar investment in making a sale—and "payout"—the profit from the sale. They are also concerned with positioning themselves and their merchandise in terms of what the customer thinks she needs rather than desires.

Where does the fashion show fit into soft goods merchandising? It is part of the carefully orchestrated presentation of merchandise to the customer to motivate her to buy. The fashion show is the means of reaching current and potential customers; the concept behind the show is the "packaging." A good fashion show planner has the ability to synthesize what is new and fashionable with what the customer wants—and then carefully promotes these looks to her.

Retailing is a multi-billion dollar business. However, given the stricter control over budgets as a result of the increasing pressure on profits, there will be less dollars available to promote fashion at a time when there is even greater need to do so. The days of fat promotional budgets for entertainment are over. The current market calls for a pragmatic and innovative approach to fashion merchandising—one that employs a knowledge of the consumer, the formula that guarantees that a promotional investment is profitable.

WHY HAVE A FASHION SHOW?

How Is a Retail Sale Made?

What goes into the purchase of a garment? Why does a woman buy a certain item? From a certain store?

Look at the elements involved: The *garment*—has an overall style or look to it, specifically composed of silhouette, fabric, texture and color, detail and price. The *retailer*—has an image or reputation, is known to the customer to carry a certain variety of styles in a range of prices, has a convenient location and is visually appealing. The *customer*—fits a demographic profile of age, income, etc.

When the elements of garment and retailer match the requirements of the customer, chances are that a sale will be made. However, the customer must get to the store, must try on the garment and where fashion is concerned—must have not only a need but a desire for it.

This is where promotion and merchandising contribute to the sale. The promotion of a fashion begins when the manufacturer shows his line to the fashion editors. The style is photographed, described, exposed—or editorialized. It is given this editorial exposure in national and local newspapers and magazines at the discretion of the fashion press—and it is advertised at the expense of the manufacturer. Stores expose the fashion further with their own national and local advertising. And on every level, the fashion is exposed with an emotional appeal that goes beyond basic description. By the time the customer comes into the store, she has a degree of familiarity with the fashion and ideally, if not a real need, a real desire for it.

And the retailer? Over and above the physical elements is the emotional appeal. Underlying every garment advertisement or promotion is the general or "institutional" message of the store to promote itself—to attract the customer.

Where does the fashion show fit in? It is essential to attract a great number of customers at one time—and to expose the fashion. The fashion show is a way of showing the style or ambience of the store as well as what fashion may be had there. It incorporates both the physical and emotional elements of a sale. The show is the means of bringing the elements—garment, retailer and customer—together. In fact, the fashion show or promotion is the only means of doing this on a broad scale. For these reasons, the fashion show is one of the most important selling tools a store has. Half the sale of a garment is made on the runway. The other half will be made later, when the customer tries it on. It is this selling aspect of a fashion show that makes it such a vital part of fashion merchandising—of retailing.

Is all this essential to putting on a fashion show? As mentioned, the overwhelming majority of fashion shows are produced by retailers for their customers. Therefore knowing the retail market and the customer and establishing a method of insuring a profitable return on the investment is critical to the success of both the fashion show and one's future, obviously, as a fashion show producer.

Even shows at the trade level, for charity, on television, as co-ops, in other words, for purposes other than building point-of-purchase sales and profits, are

15

produced to sell something, and that means insuring a match of merchandise to customer, a method of operation and a favorable ratio between "input" and "payout."

What Is a Fashion Show?

By definition, a fashion show is a presentation of merchandise on live models. A good show makes one or more general statements about fashion while at the same time shows individual and specific items to support or illustrate these comments. Furthermore the items must be authoritative, pulled together, edited by the store for the customer. And, needless to say, presented with all the drama and excitement the store and its budget can infuse into it.

These authoritative fashion statements must go beyond the garments to include accessories and beauty hints—the broad area covered by the word "fashion." And in presenting the fashion story, it must include all the elements of a good, newsworthy story:

What? . . . . specific and general fashions
Why? . . . . a critical point—motivation to buy—because the items are necessary, devastating, attractive, flattering, impart a certain chic, etc.
How? . . . . demonstrate the way to put the look together
When and where? suggest or imply the proper time and place

How do you make a point about fashion or style—particularly when fashion is of its nature—change—and people resist change. By overemphasizing or dramatizing it—not to absurdity—but so that a strong point is made. Fashion publications and even stores have sometimes been criticized for this overemphasis (or exaggeration). "Who would ever wear that!" And yet how quickly one forgets the magazine with clothes like those hanging in one's closet—or the show with looks you've been seeing on the streets for months. And when have you bought as a result of this. In fashion and retailing, to be forgettable is to be out of business.

One point in passing about the term *"style show."* Never use it. The dictionary defines "fashion" as a generic term for the prevailing style during a certain time, the word "style" is defined as a manner of expression characteristic of a particular period, school or nation. Both words refer to an individual or distinguishing manner, method or mode of doing something. However, "style show" is an old-fashioned, passé and provincial term—not yet old enough to be quaint or camp. This is reason enough not to use it—never mind the semantics.

The Purpose of the Fashion Show

The fashion show is a tool of retailing with one basic purpose—to sell merchandise. There are secondary reasons for holding a show, but the ultimate criterion for judging the show is sales. If it doesn't sell, it isn't a success.

The show must have entertainment value, of course, to hold the audience's attention. But in view of the economic outlook for the foreseeable future, the days

WHY HAVE A FASHION SHOW?

of the Cecil B. DeMille-style spectaculars are now part of history.

Over and above the selling function of the show—and directly related to sales—is the ability of the show to build traffic. Because of the nature of retailing (the need to try on) customers must come into a store as a condition for most sales. In addition, stores rely to an extent on impulse buying for a percentage of profits, and the customer must be on the scene for that. Until the human figure and apparel sizes become one hundred percent standardized, or until the retailing business becomes wholly mail order, store traffic will be vital. The ideal spot for the show therefore, is the store itself. Only for very good reasons would a show be held outside the store. Similarly, a trade show is most effective in the designer's showroom. Charity benefits, theatrical productions and other shows requiring special housing outside a store can still produce traffic and there are techniques for encouraging people into the store some time after a show. A smart retailer, if he is participating in a larger effort, will do what he can to see the show is held in his store.

Running close to the selling and traffic-building functions is the ability to inform. The show must tell the customer what is in the store at any given time. Not only showing what is new in the store, but also showing the customer how to put the new look together, how it fits into her present wardrobe. Another important aspect to consider in these days of buying clothes as investments, is to give the customer the long range view of fashion (i.e., when it was introduced, its ability to last). There are shows, as we will see later, that are promoted as informative or "how to" shows. The tenor of the commentary and merchandise centers around helping to solve specific and common problems. When the audience is sophisticated—in large cities and enclaves around the country—the show functions to reenforce their fashion ideas, rather than to present new information.

Another reason for a show might be public relations. Participation in a community project, or a store-sponsored benefit, enhances the prestige of the store and gains it a reputation for civic responsibility, in addition to giving it recognition. This goodwill has a way of encouraging customers.

A fashion show is always a good time for a store, or the sponsoring organization or firm, to display its unique qualities and tout its services. It is important that the fashions being shown truly reflect the character of the group holding the show. The taste and buying policy of a store should be reflected in the merchandise shown; the customer appeal and profitability of a manufacturer or textile firm; the attitude and significance of a civic group. It is also important to tie in a store's available services. Tell a group of young mothers about the bridal salon at a children's show? Why not—those little girls will marry some day—and buy the gown from a store they have relied on for years (and spend five or six times that amount on furnishing their new homes).

There is another more intangible function of the show that ties into retailing and sales and that is its ability to build customer loyalty. A store reflects an image in the minds of its clientele. It is associated with the merchandise it carries, a certain fashion style, a decor, a quality of service. Customers travel to the store to buy a certain item they have seen or know is there, but more often because of the store's image. The store has a style they want and they expect to find that look there. This image must be reenforced through the clothes and the presentation of them. This is especially important since the larger seasonal shows attract a certain number of people who don't normally shop there. This is the store's best chance to convert them to regular customers.

How to Evaluate Show Results

It is ironic that while a show must be evaluated on the basis of whether or not it sells, it is extremely difficult to measure the impact in exact figures.

Most fashion shows are produced with merchandise assembled from the entire store, which means that sales from the show will be equally distributed. Occasionally you will see clear-cut, concentrated results where show merchandise has been taken from a single department. But these shows do not occur regularly. Not only are sales, generated by the show, spread out over dress, sportswear, accessories, foundation departments to list a few, but because generic looks are promoted, the show will increase sales on merchandise of a similar type as well as show items. You will also find sales being made over a period of weeks following the show. Or people from the audience making purchases for others. All of this makes it nearly impossible to attribute sales directly to the show.

How do you judge results then? Many retailers reply, "If sales in general are healthy, then it's a success." However, there are ways to be a little more specific than this.

Monthly sales figures broken down by department are a great help in determining the effect of the show. Where a show is being held for the first time, or during a different time period, there should be noticeable differences in the figures. When the show is an annual event on approximately the same date, previous months' figures can be compared, after allowing for seasonal variations. This can be done for all departments represented in the show.

Another result of the show is store traffic. Again, it is virtually impossible to measure statistically. Here, it is wise to rely on the judgment of store buyers and department managers. They would have a good feel for what is developing in their departments, or whether or not there is increased activity. They can, in fact, give you estimates on specific show items that are checking out of the departments, sales activity that seems to be show-related and increased traffic.

Ideally then, you would have a combination of sales figures, plus general estimates from each department. This should be strong enough to warrant a judgment for your own and management's records.

It is not a bad idea to check unrelated departments several days after a show. It never hurts to include enthusiastic comments from the sporting goods depart-

WHY HAVE A FASHION SHOW?

ment that they enjoyed better-than-usual traffic.

And—back to the intangible aspects—if records indicate a healthy growth in sales and charge accounts among people in the store's market and beyond, and a good portion of these are coming from young people (the future backbone of the store's clientele) chances are they had been reached by the fashion show and the promotional efforts surrounding it.

A word on the store management's view of the show: the word is *profit*.

How Management Looks at the Show

Anyone planning a show must take a more pragmatic approach than they have in the past. Very simply, management figures profits on a per-square-foot basis. Lines that don't sell are phased out. A portion of the profits are allocated to efforts that generate more sales. This view should be kept in mind not only when it is time to get a budget approved for the coming year's shows, but throughout the year. It is a question of "merchandising" the shows to management on a year-round basis.

This means flagging the results of the show in memo form. And actively soliciting quotes from store personnel. Before closing the files on a show, write a follow-up memo. Particulars to include a brief description of the merchandise, location, etc., personnel involved, specific promotion and tie-ins and how they benefited the store, estimated attendance and results as specifically as possible in relation to sales, traffic and any of the intangibles.

Types of Fashion Shows | 3

Fashion shows run the gamut in size and significance from presentations that are so small they could almost be called sneak previews to presentations that are so elaborate they are closer to Broadway shows.

Most fashion shows are formal presentations. There are defined areas for the merchandise to be shown, for the audience and there is a specific sequence and pace to the merchandise. The informal show is the single exception to this. While the merchandise is selected in advance, models wander more or less at their own pace, giving information on the clothes they're wearing. There is no defined area of presentation; it could be a department, a floor or the entire store. The "audience" of course, is everywhere.

All formal fashion shows can be divided into two basic types: the fashion parade and the dramatized show. These two types can be further divided into categories, although this is somewhat arbitrary since many of the categories overlap (for instance, a seasonal show could be staged as a parade, a spectacular or possibly as an informal presentation). Also, the importance of one type of category over another will vary from one segment of the fashion industry to another. (A retailer may favor the fashion parade, while a dramatized show is produced most often by textile manufacturers or charity organizations.)

Following is a listing of the two basic types of formal shows and the categories that fall within them.

The parade is a runway presentation of merchandise in consecutive order. It is distinguished by a runway and entryway or stage area. A garment—or multiples—is shown one after the other. Models "parade" the runway at specified intervals (in fact, they may walk, run, dance, skip but follow a predetermined course down the runway).

The runway itself can be a carpet, tiers or platforms forming different patterns. The stage may be merely an entryway, an area perpendicular to the runway. Props

The fashion parade uses a defined runway area. Models—individually or in groups—follow a pre-timed and pre-determined route from entrance to exit.

The Fashion Parade

21

HOW TO PRODUCE A FASHION SHOW

Props or accessories are kept to a minimum—a tote bag, tennis racquet—to simply suggest a setting. Of all the show types, it is the most common, simplest to mount and the most adaptable.

It can be held anywhere from a department selling floor to a shopping mall or theater. The merchandise can include anything and everything. Music is a necessary part of the show. It can be recorded or live, and tied in to the general theme of the show or the item being shown. The runway area should be well lighted, although no special lighting is required. Spotlighting is a good way to dramatize the effect. Refreshments are not necessary, however, they are a good way to attract an audience, and a nice touch if the budget permits. Anything from coffee and tea to a buffet or sit-down dinner can be served. An admission fee is optional. It creates paper work, but obviously can help defray expenses.

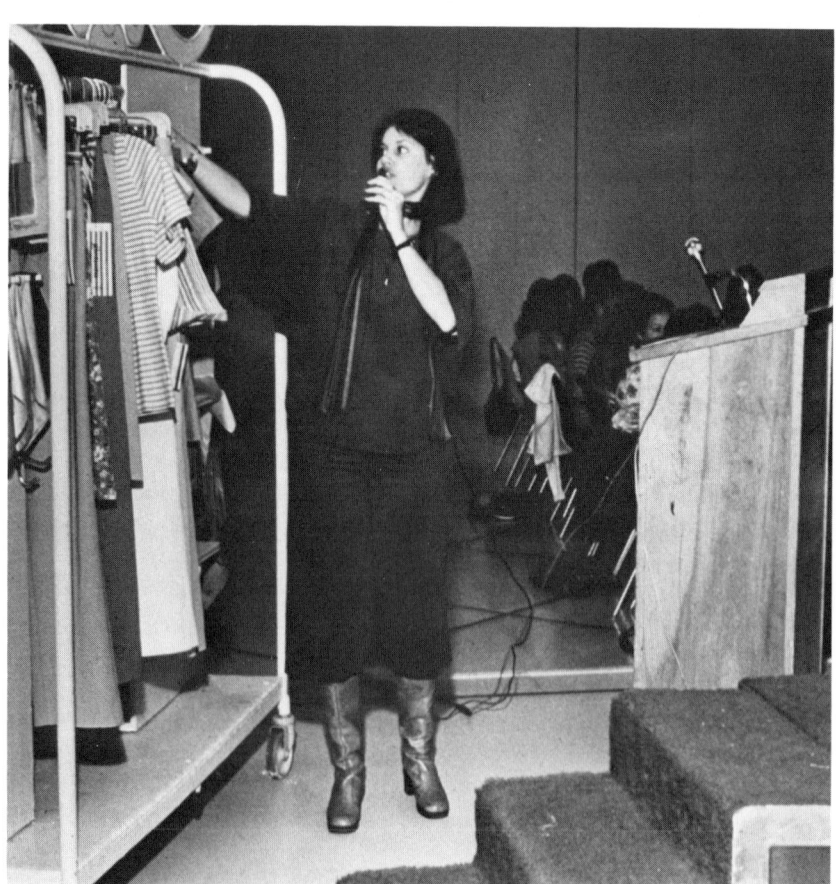

A Glamour Magazine commentator demonstrates the "how to" of wardrobe planning, part of a "More for Your Money" promotion at Rich's, Atlanta.

TYPES OF FASHION SHOWS

Types of fashion parades would include:
1. The seasonal show is the most common and generally held twice a year, at the beginning of the spring/summer and fall/winter seasons. The seasonal show attracts the largest audience and shows the broadest selection of merchandise of all the types of shows; children's wear, active sportswear and bridal wear as well as the larger areas of sportswear and dresses. (Holiday and Resort Shows, held in October and November, are also seasonal but tend to be specialized as to the audience they attract.)
2. Presentations of any of the specific ready-to-wear groups such as sportswear, dresses, coats and suits, career clothes.
3. Specialty shows are any shows involving merchandise which appeals to a small group of people with unique interests. Specialty markets would include children's wear, men's wear, bridal wear, active sportswear, maternity, home sewing or any other small merchandise category. Most require a knowledge of technical details, such as home sewing where the latest designer techniques may be highlighted. Others require an adaptation of basic planning such as the extra supervision necessary for a children's show. The bridal show requires both special knowledge (the intricacies of etiquette) and special planning (tie-ins with housewares, luggage and other areas a bride-to-be would be interested in).
4. Co-op shows, in which several firms organize, underwrite or participate in the presentation.
5. Trunk shows where the show is organized in one location and clothes (with or without models or commentator) are "trunked" around and presented in other locations.
6. Designer shows which feature the clothes of one, or occasionally more than one, designer exclusively.
7. Charity events which are staged for the purpose of raising funds.
8. Trade shows which are presented by one segment of the fashion industry for another, i.e., apparel manufacturers for retail buyers, fiber companies for mills.
9. Televised or taped shows are generally presented in parade form although the film may be edited later to illustrate certain points.

The Dramatized Show

The dramatized presentation has an extra dimension added. Fashion points or whole concepts are illustrated rather than just shown. The purpose is to create impact. This can be done by demonstrating a particular concept, showing how a look is achieved or adapted through the use of entertainment or special staging, backdrops and scenery, action and dialogue, music and dancing.

HOW TO PRODUCE A FASHION SHOW

Model answers shopper's questions during informal showing at Saks Fifth Avenue, New York.

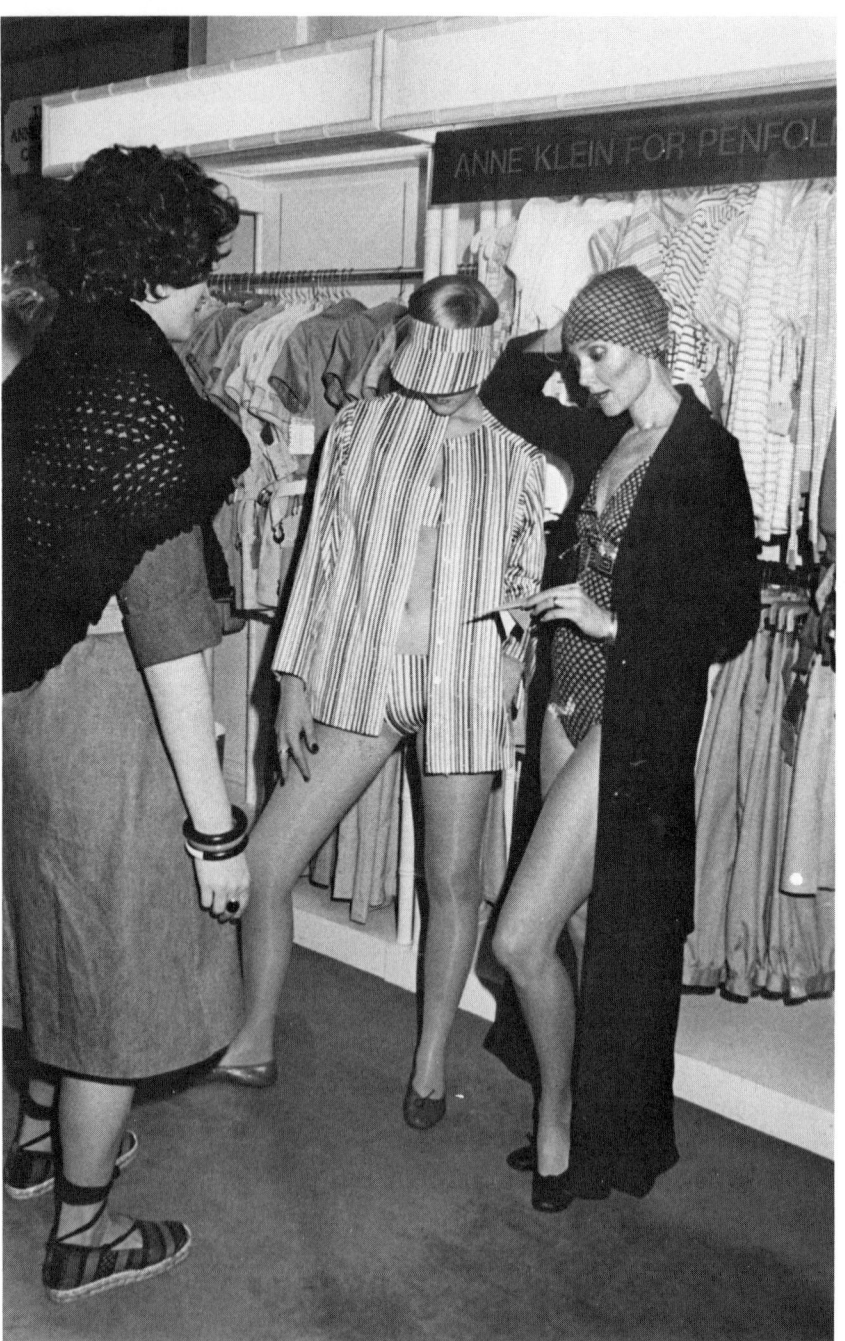

TYPES OF FASHION SHOWS

Types of dramatized shows would include:
1. The spectacular is the most elaborate fashion show. Fabulous backdrops, skits, music, singing and dancing or dialogue can be used to entertain and amuse as well as to make important fashion points. It can be extremely sophisticated. Because of the difficulty and cost in mounting the spectacular it is generally used as a charity event or as a major "event" to create publicity and excitement for a manufacturer, textile firm or retailer. It may require special personnel, extra training for models or performers and heavy promotion. This type of show should never be considered unless the sales or contributions will justify the enormous production expense.
2. The "how to" show informs and instructs the audience about new or established fashion ideas. It may demonstrate how older women can conceal figure faults or how teens can use several basic pieces and accessories to create an entire wardrobe. The demonstration aspect is emphasized over the fashion presentation. This type of show is generally suited to a less sophisticated or less knowledgeable audience.
3. The "hatbox" or "bandbox" show is a good way to utilize a small area and budget. A single person models each outfit, moving behind a screen to change while a running commentary is maintained the entire time.

Many of the categories covered under fashion parades may be staged as dramatized shows, and vice versa. Seasonal shows may take the form of spectaculars; any of the major ready-to-wear categories lend themselves as well. A couture show could be both a spectacular and a parade. The home sewing show could be staged as a "how to" or as a "hatbox" show, as could many others.

The Informal Show

The informal show is neither a parade nor a dramatized presentation; it is a "casual" presentation. Although structure and time are not as important as in a parade, many of the preparations are similar.

The informal showing consists of a few models who make an appearance at periodic intervals carrying cards with descriptive information. The purpose is to show the fresh merchandise that has come into the store between seasons, to advertise a newly created department, a small designer collection or to show a special group of fashions when there is not enough interest to warrant a full-scale presentation. Merchandise categories that might be presented informally include: active sportswear, resort wear, couture clothes, evening clothes.

The informal show may stand alone or it may be scheduled in conjunction with a designer's appearance or following a large, formal fashion show in order to reach people who might have missed the original event.

While merchandise is planned and pulled, the preparations are far looser than for a formal show. The fashion coordinator might instruct the two or three

HOW TO PRODUCE A FASHION SHOW

models she has booked to pull about four or five newly arrived pieces from the sportswear department and show them on the main floor.

Informal showings might be scheduled in the store's restaurant or within a single department. Wherever the location, it is the least expensive and easiest way to present a group of fashions.

Background and Advance Planning | 4

A tremendous amount of advance planning goes into producing a fashion show, even when the clothes are provided by an outside source. A master plan must be set up and executed—but there are decisions to be made even before this can be worked out.

Planning a fashion show means working backwards from the audience. Since the goal is to sell, it is really the audience who decides the success or failure of the show. If the show doesn't motivate the audience to buy, it is a waste of time and money. A magnificent couture show, exquisitely staged, has very little impact on women who are customers for budget dresses. Wonderful entertainment but hardly profitable. By the same token, working women wouldn't buy young junior clothes—would in fact, yawn through a teen show. This situation can not only be unproductive, it can actually do damage. A couture customer seeing a budget show could assume the store is definitely not for her—that customer is lost until something specific is done to lure her back. By the same token, a charity organization would find it nearly impossible to get a retailer to co-sponsor a fashion show if previous ones failed to produce sales. And an apparel manufacturer wouldn't survive many seasons without attracting the right buyers. Every store, group or company has to overcome a certain amount of "threshold resistance" from certain potential customers—a fashion show should relieve it rather than create it.

A show commonly attracts a mixed audience, rather than one wholly unsuited. Attracting a few people who may be uninterested in buying is unavoidable, more than a few means there's been a miscalculation.

The exception to this, of course, is the seasonal presentation. A mixed audience is desirable since the newly arrived merchandise appeals to everyone. Audience and show are matched up—"something for everyone."

The audience/show match-up works both ways. Starting with the audience

The Audience as Starting Point

A hotel ballroom captures the mood of a wedding reception. Here, a Jordan Marsh, Florida, Bridal Show in conjunction with The Bride's Magazine.

who will attend, you tailor the show to them. Conversely, you can tailor a show to attract the audience you want to attend.

Learning the Market Area

Where does one learn about the audience? Each store, charity, manufacturer has a market area. The market area is the surrounding geographic region from which a potential audience will be drawn. With a store, regions vary widely in size from a fifty-mile radius—larger in sparsely populated areas—to a few city blocks—in densely populated areas. The market area may overlap that of another store, which creates a healthy competitive situation. Within this market area, are customers who find the store convenient to travel to, or who will make the extra effort to get to if convinced of finding attractive merchandise, attractively priced.

An apparel manufacturer's market area includes the geographic areas where he has—or wishes—distribution; his audience is the retail buyers who represent the stores in the target areas.

A charity group's market area would include a single community or neighborhood, usually any group who will either benefit from the fund-raising or who are active supporters of a common cause within the community. Well-known local or national personalities can extend the drawing power of the event.

Within this geographic market area there exists a broad cross section of potential customers. In some cases, a homogenous population exists: a concentration of high and low income families, senior citizens, singles, etc. In these cases a store or an organization is already geared to the audience. The store is merchandised for the specific group it serves and advance planning in terms of audience-tailoring will obviously vary little from show to show.

In most cases, however, the market area will be made up of different groups of people with different demographic profiles. It is up to the show coordinator to know these groups—what percentage fall into each of the various age groups, income levels, occupations; what are the leisure time activities; where concentrations of these groups exist within the area as a whole; what percentage of each group consistently shops in the store; who shops infrequently, or not at all.

It is helpful to put this information together with census tracts and business bureau statistics. For instance, if the area population is increasing, are they families or singles? Is the store's business increasing with the population? What age are the children? Are the new people near retirement age? Is the store catering to this new influx of groups? Are small shops on the increase? Or large chains? Or specialty stores? What advantages can the store offer—which can be promoted via the show—that the new competitors can't? Is the market area becoming predominately a farming or mining community, subject to special economic fluctuations. These are the types of questions and information that should be discussed with store management and factored into show planning.

Statistics and reports issued by industry associations are valuable, too. For instance anyone who saw the U.S. Lawn Tennis Association's report on the

BACKGROUND AND ADVANCE PLANNING

Inventive Site: Ivey's Teen Show on ice in a shopping center mall. (Courtesy of Ivey's, Charlotte, North Carolina and Seventeen *Magazine.*)

HOW TO PRODUCE A FASHION SHOW

The main aisle becomes a runway for an L.S. Ayres branch store presentation. (Courtesy of Glamour *Magazine.)*

increasing interest in tennis in 1971 (projecting a 300% increase in tennis players between 1971 and 1980) would have known to develop business in this area. And the fashion show is one of the best ways to do it.

With statistics revealing discernible trends in hobbies, sports, travel, it is possible to anticipate a demand, or fan the flames of interest by promoting it at the show.

The fashion presentation must be consistent with the goals of the store as well. One can't go too far wrong in a general way: the merchandise itself is bought with a general look at a price that buyers and management assume will sell within the market area. If store buying policy emphasizes styling and low prices this would be reflected in the show. If high fashion is the store's strength, or an emphasis is placed on personalized service, these policies would be incorporated into the show.

BACKGROUND AND ADVANCE PLANNING

In addition, many department stores today are actively engaged in pushing their market areas outward, seeking new customers, motivating current ones to heavier purchases. Most have researched their markets and know where new business will come from. The fashion show is an excellent way to draw these customers into the store and a special effort should be made to reach them and convert them—through the show—to regular customers.

How do you go about attracting an audience? In general, by gearing the merchandise, its presentation and promotion to the audience you wish to attract. Promotion is the key—put together with a knowledge of the potential audience that exists. Specific methods will be covered in later chapters, but show information can be directed to any specific group within the total market area. If a general audience is desired, one would start with current customers—through signs and placards within the store, and invitations to regular customers. One can purchase mailing lists by zip code and broaden the audience by inviting people who don't normally patronize the store. Television, radio and newspaper announcements will alert a broad cross section of the populace as well. Or one can target in on a specialized group. For instance, an active sportswear show can be promoted via information disseminated through the active sportswear and sporting goods departments, local pro shops, mailings to pro shop customer lists, sports and country clubs, an ad in the sports section of the local paper, or during a broadcast of a sporting event. A bridal show on the other hand can be promoted through the bridal, housewares and related departments, mailings to brides-to-be registered with the store, with a local jeweler, florist, or from newspaper announcements and from lists accumulated in the bridal department.

Attracting the Right Audience

How does one limit an audience? In terms of the interest of the audience, the way it is promoted, and where, will tend to exclude uninterested groups. People who don't sew, won't make the effort to attend a sewing show. And if the promotion is confined to the piece goods department, piece goods ads in newspapers and various specific lists, it isn't likely to lure customers of ready-to-wear.

Controlling the size of an audience is also possible. The ideal is a full house—neither too crowded nor with too many gaping, empty seats. Promotion via media reaching a huge number of people guarantees a large response. One can limit the size by issuing tickets in limited quantities with a definite cutoff number.

The audience directly or indirectly determines every aspect of the show. It determines the type of presentation: an informal showing is preferable when the interest is minimal or scattered; a formal presentation for a larger audience.

For example, a limited group of fresh merchandise that has arrived at the store in the middle of the season might be shown informally, whereas large groups of merchandise covering many ready-to-wear categories that have arrived in the beginning of a season would be shown formally. A "how to" show might be the

HOW TO PRODUCE A FASHION SHOW

Plants and folding screens form a simple backdrop for a Lord & Taylor in-store show. (Courtesy of Lord & Taylor and The Bride's *Magazine.)*

An auditorium will draw large numbers of customers into the store, yet the show will not disrupt selling activities on the various floors. (Courtesy of Rich's, Atlanta and Glamour *Magazine.)*

BACKGROUND AND ADVANCE PLANNING

most effective way to reach older women with a fashion message about up-dating their wardrobes. A fast-paced parade without commentary for working women or sophisticated couture customers who have a limited amount of time or have acquired the fashion savvy to grasp the implications of the fashion message quickly.

In addition to the promotion, merchandise and presentation, the audience determines the timing and location of the show, since it must meet their needs, as well.

The type and size of the audience also determines the location. However, since the purpose of having the show is to sell, and this is encouraged by bringing people into the store and allowing them to try on the merchandise, the ideal location is within the store.

The selling floor is an especially good location when the majority of the fashions to be shown are taken from nearby departments. A broad main aisle, a single department or several departments together are also suitable for a formal show. (Avoid using a long narrow main aisle with small separate departments opening off it. The audience seated in various sections sees an awkward and disjointed presentation.) Floor stands, racks and moveable counters can be shifted to accommodate folding chairs. Many moderate-sized stores have been able to seat up to five hundred people in this manner. Assuming the show is held during regular business hours, and provided it doesn't disrupt other areas, it's an excellent means of producing traffic and can be held on any floor. If the store is closed for business, it's best to hold the show on the main floor, and for security reasons, rope and confine traffic to the immediate area.

The disadvantage to this arrangement is the lack of facilities, i.e., dressing rooms, electrical outlets, also a backdrop and entryway would necessarily be simplified under the circumstances. There are however, ways to set up a dressing room, provided the other facilities exist or can be "imported" for the occasion, as we will see later. Of course, a large audience will automatically eliminate the small in-store sites.

A community room or an auditorium is another prime area, with the capacity to seat more people comfortably, with proper facilities at hand and without disrupting departmental activity. In addition most are equipped with a stage, public address system and special lighting equipment.

If the store has a restaurant, this can be used, too, with a platform or stage set up at one end. If refreshments are served, arrangements should be made to halt service during the show, to avoid distraction.

An in-store show has overwhelming advantages. Occasionally there are compelling reasons for holding a show outside the store, advantages that offset the loss of immediate traffic and store identification you achieve with an in-store show. An extremely large audience would necessitate holding the show outside the

The Location of the Show

store, as would the need to serve alcoholic beverages if the store has no license. A spectacular, an elaborate luncheon, cocktail or dinner party or a show combined with a party, dance or other form of entertainment might strain the store's facilities. In this case it could be held at a local woman's club, country club or theater. It is possible to be quite inventive about locations: a racetrack club house is one possibility; a discotheque (closed to the public) is another; a large ferry boat or side-wheeler; a public park or garden; a museum. Any place that's accessible, with the necessary facilities is suitable—if it's innovative it lends a certain excitement to the show. Other suitable areas might include the school auditorium for a teen or university show. Shopping center malls can be used so that the show can be situated near the store. A filmed or taped show can be presented most easily in a studio, but could also be shot anywhere the equipment will go. Plans and invitations for outdoor shows should include a rain date for obvious reasons.

Gearing the site to audience size and tastes is another argument for knowing the audience in advance.

Show Timing   Again the overriding consideration must be the audience. The time of year, the day of the week and the time of day to hold the fashion show will all be determined by the needs of the audience.

Fashion shows are usually presented at the very beginning of a season for two reasons. First, new merchandise pours into the store prior to the season during which it is sold. Spring and summer merchandise is bought in October and November for delivery in February, March and April; fall and winter merchandise is bought in May and June for August and September delivery. Apparel market timing continues to blur and overlap, but these months still remain the biggest for buying and delivering. After the merchandise is unpacked and ticketed, it goes out on the floor. It is then promoted—the fashion show being one way. The show is then coordinated with the general buying and merchandising efforts.

The second reason to hold a fashion show at the beginning of a season is that when the weather changes customers are just beginning to think about changing their wardrobes to suit it. They are far more responsive to fashion promotion at this time when months of different occasions and activities stretch out in front of them. This is a time of evaluating the new fashion message, of planning a wardrobe around it, of shopping the stores and magazines for ideas, of fitting new styles into existing wardrobes. This is the period of greatest expenditure with fill-ins, replacements and last minute buying excursions.

To take advantage of the consumer's frame of mind, spring shows would be scheduled in February or March; fall shows, September or October. Despite the fact that a great deal of merchandise now is year-round or multi-seasonal, to a certain extent, holidays will trigger buying activities. Easter, for instance, is usually the kickoff for spring buying, although this varies from year to year, since

BACKGROUND AND ADVANCE PLANNING

Easter is a "moveable feast." Memorial Day is a signal for summer—leftover from the days when women never wore white shoes before May 31, also the date for men to break out their white dinner jackets. Labor Day is the fall turning point; again from bygone days when following this date one wore dark cottons. Labor Day remains the last official summer weekend, after which families return from vacations or weekend houses and begin preparing for the colder months and school—which makes it ideal timing for back-to-school shows.

October and November are good months for holiday and resort promotions. This "mini-season" is handled differently by stores. It is sometimes promoted as part of the fall and winter merchandise and included in that show; it might also be shown via informal showings. Over the past few years this mini-season has increased in importance for both stores and manufacturers as a means of determining in advance what the consumer will react to the following spring. Often manufacturers will introduce and stores will test what they believe will be big new spring/summer looks. For this reason, or because there is heavy consumer interest, holiday and resort shows can be staged formally during this period.

About four to six weeks into the new season, informal modeling is often done showing "fresheners"—items that have been bought after or in between the periods of heavy activity. This happens because customers can grow bored once they feel they've seen all that's available for a given season. Manufacturers know this and provide new merchandise for buyers usually every six weeks. It's rare for a store to mount a formal show for these items—the interest doesn't justify it and while it could generate some customer traffic, particularly during the dead deep-summer and January periods, most stores build traffic via off-price promotions.

Although other things are taken into consideration, the day of the week and time of day are also set according to audience preference.

By scheduling an in-store show during peak traffic periods, you can boost attendance. You will attract people who regularly shop in the store at the time of the show and who have planned in advance to combine their shopping with attending the show. You will also catch people who happen to be shopping at the time of the show and will stop to watch. If you're looking for the largest possible exposure for the show, this is the way to do it. The scheduling must always be based on a knowledge of customer activities, preferences and store traffic patterns.

When do customers shop? We've already seen that the beginning of each season is the best time to introduce new fashions. The worst time in terms of customers' buying trends is the July and August period when many are on vacation. December and January are generally poor due to heavy social activity and "economic recovery." The months prior to these are good, since people "stock up" for future events.

As to which day of the week to hold the show for the most part you can rule

Ohrbach's presentation of line-for-line copies of European designs attracts a knowledgeable, sophisticated audience. Pace and commentary are upbeat. (Wide World Photos, Inc.)

35

out Sunday. Sunday shows have worked once in a while, in small communities, during a transition of seasons when weekend activities are not yet in full swing. But usually Sunday is taken seriously as a day of rest. Saturday mornings and afternoons are good shopping periods and can be taken advantage of. Mondays and Friday are not considered prime times: Monday is a weekend recovery day and Friday is a weekend preparation day. Therefore Tuesday, Wednesday, Thursday and Saturday are the best days to hold shows.

As to what time the show should be held depends again on the audience. Women with part-time or full-time jobs have to be accommodated at lunch time, after five or on weekends. Stores open late Mondays and/or Thursdays can consider this time as well. Mothers of young children would want a show during school hours—or if it's a children's show, after school or on Saturday. Evening and Saturday shows encourage men to attend. Fashion shows for older women whose families have grown, or women with a great deal of leisure time, can be scheduled on weekdays, mid-mornings or afternoons. Knowing storewide traffic patterns, as well as being able to break traffic patterns down by department, helps immensely in the scheduling process.

For an out-of-store show, the same criteria applies. Peak traffic periods are good times to take advantage of since you know your audience is available. A knowledge of their activities helps you avoid conflicts with their plans, too.

Another "time" geared to the audience is the length and pace of the show. In general, the length of time during which the fashions are presented in a store show should run between thirty and forty-five minutes. Allowing fifteen to twenty minutes for the introduction, close, credits and giveaways, the total show should run between forty-five minutes and an hour. But the fashion portion for a general audience should never exceed forty-five minutes. Retailers are often tempted to pack in everything that's new, thinking that if they show enough something will strike a chord with everyone in the audience. An audience's attention span is limited. Once you've gone over forty-five minutes (and that is the maximum time, fashion-wise), you've lost your audience. They are incapable of absorbing any more. Show coordinators must develop confidence in their ability to edit the merchandise to include the best representative selection and to stick with it, resisting the temptation to add an outfit here and there.

The other timing involved is the pace of the show. In general, a show should be paced to present one or two outfits per minute. This is the time during which the average audience focuses attention on the outfit. Once again, the specific audience will determine the actual pace of the show. The more sophisticated the audience, the faster the pace. The "how to" show mentioned earlier would be paced more slowly to allow for description plus information about how the look is put together, how figure faults can be concealed, or whatever the "how to" is concentrated around. A single outfit could take several minutes. A show for younger people would be paced faster, to hold their attention. As would a seasonal

BACKGROUND AND ADVANCE PLANNING

or higher-priced show, or import collection—or any show for a knowledgeable group. For faster paced shows, outfits could be spaced fifteen to thirty seconds apart, or presented in multiples without commentary or commentated in groups. The audience registers a more general impression with a faster pace. This makes good sense in view of the fact that the show is presenting generic rather than specific fashion. Many manufacturers when showing a major line, show well over a hundred pieces in thirty to forty-five minutes. This kind of fast pacing is geared to fashion professionals—store buyers and press. If you are showing two pieces or more per minute, it's critical that you maintain the pace—lags in this show could mean a two-hour presentation.

The Planning Meeting

Many stores set up annual meetings to determine the fashion show schedule for the entire year. An executive committee will determine the number of shows, the departments, markets or designers to be promoted, a general timetable and the budget for each. Magazines and manufacturers may operate the same way and base the number of shows on the overall budget. If this is the case, then the planning meeting for an individual show is a little easier with the big questions answered.

Who coordinates the fashion show? In a store, it could be the fashion coordinator, promotion director or special events director to name a few. A textile or

Bloomingdale's fashion staff decides the fashion theme and divides responsibilities for an upcoming show.

HOW TO PRODUCE A FASHION SHOW

The Responsibility Sheet is routed to everyone concerned with the show. Job deadlines can be listed and final costs can be added later to simplify bookkeeping.

```
                    Responsibility Sheet

Event: _____          Memo To: (Individual names
Place: _____                   would be listed, and checked
Date:  _____                   if they receive this memo)
Time:  _____          President
                                 Vice-President
                                 Advertising Director
Invitations:                     Promotion/Publicity
                                   Director
    Mailing List_____  Special Events Director
    Order Invitations_____  Display Director
    Address Envelopes_____  General Manager
    Mail (Stamps)_____   Divisional Managers
    In-store Invitations_____  Department Managers
    Press Invitations_____  Print Shop
                                 Maintenance
Fashion Show:                    Others:

    Book Models_____   Photography:
    Book Dressers_____
    Fitting Date_____       Pre-Event _____
    Accessories_____       At Event  _____
    Rehearsal Date_____       Press Releases _____
    Trucking Clothes_____       Press List _____

Hotel/Store Arrangements:        Miscellaneous:

    Book Room for Show_____       Special Mailings _____
    Book Room for Out-of-Town        Advertising _____
      Personnel_____       Thank You Notes _____
    Flowers or Gift for
      Commentator/Designer_____
    Food_____
    Liquor_____
    Decor/Flowers_____
    Lights_____
    Runway & Construction____
    Microphone_____
    Racks, Hangers, Mirrors,
      Tables, etc._____
    Chairs_____
    Security_____
    Giveaways_____
    Music_____
```

apparel manufacturer or a magazine would use a merchandise or fashion director. Titles are not so important. What is important, is that anyone, even an independent organization or charity, should use a coordinator who knows about fashion, knows the firm, and has the ability to manage people. This last talent is important since even a small informal showing requires working with other people, assigning duties and then making sure the job is performed. (An elaborate show may require the services of a free-lance producer without any knowledge of fashion. He would rely on the fashion coordinator, or someone in that capacity, to make merchandise decisions and give advice on key points to be emphasized.) The first step the show producer takes is to set up a planning meeting for the fashion show.

The meeting is the first step in coordinating and executing the show. The meeting on an informal show could consist of the coordinator and a model. The more elaborate the show, the larger the meeting. A spectacular needn't include everyone at the outset but decisions should be made on who is to be brought in from outside to work on the show.

BACKGROUND AND ADVANCE PLANNING

The show planning meeting is set up six weeks to three months in advance of the show. Some of the basic show questions should have already been answered. The general merchandise category should already be established (seasonal, couture, sportswear, etc.), also the target audience. This in turn determines the general location (based on size). The basic type of show will have been determined by the other information as well as when and where the show will be held. When the audience, merchandise and show allow for some flexibility, the exact presentation will be determined during the meeting. For example, whether to present a teen show as a "how to" or a straightforward parade.

When these questions are settled, a meeting is held to determine specific aspects of the show such as a list of jobs and who will be responsible for each job and the time schedule for completion. The meeting serves as a brainstorming session. The coordinator, staff and all or some of the personnel from the involved departments will discuss and decide the options.

The basic fashion message (policy, position, viewpoint) can be decided at this time. Also the specific theme of the show will be worked out—this could mean coming up with a basic concept and letting the art and copy people go to work on it. (It's helpful to keep a file on ideas for themes and add to it during the year.) It could mean getting as specific as a title and working out a color scheme. Color scheme and graphics are part of the show planning and should be defined and used consistently on all advertising and promotional materials—the display and decor must also reflect the theme.

The audience should be zeroed in on in terms of type and size. And a definite strategy worked out to promote the show via advertising and, where necessary, direct mail.

If it's to be a parade, decisions can be made on the exact way of showing, i.e., pivots, dancing, fast walk.

How elaborate the stage and backdrop will be is also determined. And whether or not to serve refreshments or include entertainment; to sell tickets; what promotional tie-ins are available; what type of music to have; who will commentate the show; who will introduce the commentator; the type of commentary.

The length of the show and pace will determine the approximate number of pieces—which in turn determines the number of models to be booked. The type of model being used—amateur, with some degree of experience, professional—will determine the number of rehearsals. A time for the final or dress rehearsal will be fixed but complicated routines or inexperienced models will require extra practice sessions. The availability of promotional tie-ins with manufacturers, magazines and other firms should be investigated and chosen as well. More often this should be arranged at the end of the year for the following year's shows, to guarantee availability and determine in advance any requirements that must be fulfilled.

The next step is to draw up a *Responsibility Sheet* which lists the jobs that

Shopping bags form a simple, effective backdrop for a Glamour *Magazine tie-in promotion with Rich's, Atlanta.*

HOW TO PRODUCE A FASHION SHOW

need to be done. Broad categories are listed such as Printing, Hotel or Store Arrangements, Promotion, Fashion Show, Advertising. Each category is then broken down into specific jobs. For instance, under Fashion Show, you can list: Book models, Book dressers, Fitting date, Rehearsals, Pull garments, Accessories. (See illustration on page 38 for more specifics.)

The Responsibility Sheet should list the name of the person who will be responsible for the job and its deadline. The sheet should be circulated to each department involved in the show. Even if outside directors, choreographers, designers are employed, someone on staff should be responsible for seeing that the job is completed.

The show coordinator, depending on the size of the show, will delegate a great deal—or a little—responsibility to others. Regardless of what jobs are delegated, the ultimate responsibility rests on the coordinator. Follow-up on jobs and deadlines is vital—if anything is forgotten or left undone, it's the coordinator's problem.

The following chapters contain all the elements for putting together a fashion show. Together they represent a check list for show planning, and each aspect should be covered on the Responsibility Sheet. As a whole the Responsibility Sheet, with its categories, forms a blueprint or master plan on how to produce a fashion show.

Planning the Merchandise: Garments and Accessories | 5

The planning of actual show merchandise begins about six weeks prior to the show date. Decisions and ideas are usually made by the fashion coordinator or planner, and the fashion staff. This can be done during the planning meeting if it is basically a fashion staff meeting, or a separate meeting can be set up later specifically to decide on show merchandise.

The decisions about merchandise are based on solid fashion knowledge and current information. Anyone making these decisions must know fashion in general, current trends and specific looks; what the store is buying and what the store is—or wants to be—known for. All this, in addition to knowing audience tastes and desires.

If the show is to be given for the trade, the primary source of information is the firm's designer. The designer will know what looks are the most important and what the firm's major retail accounts are most interested in seeing. Often, an apparel manufacturer will invite key accounts to preview a line prior to the seasonal opening to get their opinions. Certain styles that seem less likely to sell will be eliminated then, with more getting the axe after the line opens. The designer or showroom personnel can advise on what the initial buyer reaction is and what looks should be well represented.

Fashion shows are presentations of current merchandise. Fashion itself is in a constant state of change. Despite the fact that a general look or feeling may predominate for one, two or three years, each season has its own version and it should be recognized. It is important to have a general fashion awareness and background in selecting merchandise. To know not only the general look that's current, but how long it has been around, what the new variations are. And now more than ever, while there may be one look that is important, there are usually other separate and distinct looks that play a minor role in the current world of fashion. For instance, in a season when the trend is toward many pieces layered

Planning the Merchandise

A model pulls the merchandise she'll show informally.

Sources of Fashion Information

41

HOW TO PRODUCE A FASHION SHOW

over each other, the one-piece jumpsuit may also be significant. Also, there are always ideas afloat which may later catch on in a big way. They may eventually develop into big trends, or be confined to fads or hot items.

Despite its waning importance, Paris is still an excellent source of basic information—both for couture and ready-to-wear. Not only do the looks spawned there find their way into all levels of the American ready-to-wear market, but it is a meeting place for American manufacturers, retail merchandise management and buyers; and because of this, the Paris market is well covered in the press. Firsthand knowledge of Parisian—and European—fashion is ideal.

The trade press runs a solid second as the best means of keeping informed. The press not only reviews important lines, it usually evaluates their importance and reports on retailers' opinions.

Together they form a consensus that is an excellent source of current information. In this way, one can become familiar with new styles, silhouettes, colors. Furthermore, each time a designer introduces a new line, it contains both authoritative statements on fashion and "straws in the wind." The authoritative look is major and significant, with the fashion reputation of the designer behind it. The "straws in the wind" are one or more looks in a different vein from the others. They are minor and the designer is, in a sense, throwing them out for comment. If they cause excitement and interest, they may develop into the big looks of the coming season. If not, they will quietly disappear into obscurity. Generally, the reaction in the press tells you how much coverage to give each look.

This holds true for American ready-to-wear in New York, Los Angeles, Dallas and the other regional apparel markets as well. Firsthand knowledge is ideal, and most fashion coordinators do attend these showings. The trade press adds a certain perspective. A discussion with the store merchandise management and buyers will give you their opinion on what is right for the store, what is being bought and why. (This will help you coordinate merchandise and audience since buyers work on their own knowledge and instinct for what will generate interest within the store's market area.)

The second step in putting together show merchandise takes place within the store. Daily visits to the stock room as merchandise arrives is the best way to stay on top of new merchandise. Familiarity with the stock over a period of time will give you a good idea of what is this season's version of a popular look introduced several seasons ago, and what is a radical departure from anything that was shown earlier. How long a look has been around and the attitude of the retailing world toward it is vital in determining what importance it should have and exactly how much exposure to give it in the show.

This holds true for specific ready-to-wear areas, the individual markets, as well as individual looks and trends. For instance, skirts with a particular line might be important. Equally important would be knowing that shape is going to be more important in dresses rather than skirts; or that the trend may be away from

If pulled merchandise is organized on racks in a single location, the run-off can be worked more quickly.

PLANNING THE MERCHANDISE: GARMENTS AND ACCESSORIES

sportswear or separates and toward dresses or ensembles.

The store's fashion image must be taken into consideration as well. If it's known for "a great look at a price," then this will be reflected in the inventory and the show. If it's middle-of-the-road, fashion- and price-wise, then this will be emphasized. If the store is known to have something for everyone, than a cross section of clothes will be represented. Obviously the individual show being planned counts, too. The biggest cross section is incorporated into the seasonal show, while smaller, more specialized shows will concentrate on and feature the smaller ready-to-wear areas or price ranges.

Perhaps most important of all, the audience you want to attract must be taken into consideration. A broad-based general audience demands that all types of looks, super-chic and not-so-new, be represented in a variety of price ranges. Audiences who are predominately affluent or thrifty will determine pricing concentration. And again, a conservative area will better appreciate a conservative fashion show—keeping in mind, however, that merchandise must be fresh and new looking, although not necessarily extreme.

Every show has a basic line or theme that is carried through. This is an umbrella under which the fashions are presented. The theme must be specific and strong enough to hold the show together. It must also be broad and cover all the merchandise categories to be shown. Specifics of silhouette, color, fabric or texture can be ruled out immediately. None are strong enough to hold the show together. While shape is often the key ingredient in a seasonal fashion message, it is difficult to come up with a promotable title. A show can contain a hundred-odd pieces, all wide or all narrow, but it is virtually impossible to invent a descriptive title dealing with shape that is exciting and that will attract the attention of the audience or the local fashion editors.

Deciding the Theme

Color is equally impractical. Not only is a monochromatic show boring and ludicrous, no season is confined to a single color area. Even when pastels predominate, there is always a bright color or two for balance and variety. Fabric and texture is also generally varied, but not interesting enough to attract attention.

The best theme contains the essence of the current fashion feeling or ambience. Feeling is a good word for it, since it should be phrased and executed (in terms of merchandise shown), in a way that generates an emotional response. It should be a phrase or term that reflects the fashion mood plus the current approach on the part of the audience to fashion in general. This is easier than one might think, since fashion doesn't exist in a vacuum, but reflects the current state of mind and affairs.

As one gains experience, it becomes easier to capture the feeling of fashion and turn it into a workable theme. Even if nothing satisfactory comes to mind immediately, one can come up with a generic phrase and use it as a working title. As the collection of merchandise takes shape, the exact title can be developed.

HOW TO PRODUCE A FASHION SHOW

The Ideal Chart ensures that all basic merchandise categories are covered and that all important looks are represented. This sample Chart indicates the 100 pieces that will be pulled in various categories for a seasonal show lasting 50 minutes (50 pieces).

```
                         Ideal Chart


Sportswear -- 30 pieces              Suits -- 15 pieces

   Shirts & tops - tailored blouse,     Chanel type
      sweater sets, halters, tanks,     Cardigan jacket
      body shirts                       Pleated/flared skirt
   Jackets - fitted, box, peacoat,      Belted jacket
      double-breasted, cropped          Double-breasted
   Skirts - pleated, flared, bias       Single-breasted
      cut, ankle-length                 Evening suits
   Pants - flared, straight leg,
      hi-rise waist, pajama type     Evening Looks -- 15 pieces

Dresses -- 20 pieces                    Glitter looks
                                        Long skirts - pleated, flared,
   A-line - belted, tent, princess         mid-calf, ankle-length
   Dress & jacket combination           Sheer tops - blouses, halters
   Shirtdress                           Palazzo pajamas
   Wrap dress                           Velvet jeans
   Two-piece look                       Plunging necklines
   Blouson top                          At-home looks
   Coat dress
                                     Children -- 10 pieces
Coats -- 10 pieces
                                        School clothes - overalls,
   Wrap coat                               T-shirts, wash-and-wear
   Fur trims                               dresses and pants
   Big top coats                        Party looks - pinafores, sheer
   Rain coats                              dresses, long dresses
   All-weather coats                    Separates - mix 'n' match,
   Reversibles                             coordinated, animal prints
   Belted coats
```

A good place to start developing a theme is to come up with a single word that epitomizes the current fashion trend or mood. Barring this, one can borrow or adapt a phrase from the trade or consumer fashion publications. Despite the fact that most retailers have a copy department capable of developing a title or headline to use, most planners will need to supply the kernel of an idea—specific direction to guide the copywriters. The ability to identify a central motif to work with is important.

If the theme is broad enough, specific merchandise will be covered comfortably. Keep in mind that the theme should be flexible and include dresses, coats, suits and other categories. Also one's approach should be flexible; don't eliminate a group of fashions simply because they don't readily fit into the theme. One can always show them as variations—interesting counterpoints to the main thrust. Rarely do you find a group of hard-edged fashion looks in the midst of soft romantic ones. But you might find tailored looks amid a season of unstructured, flowing fashions. By all means include them. Each will serve to dramatize and point up the characteristics of the other, and will add needed variety to the show.

PLANNING THE MERCHANDISE: GARMENTS AND ACCESSORIES

How Much to Show

The rule of thumb is at least one piece per minute, and more if the audience is sophisticated. The fashion portion of the show should not exceed forty-five minutes, with total start to finish time, including introduction, close, credits, etc., not exceeding an hour. A seasonal show with a large varied audience could take the maximum time of an hour. Allowing fifteen minutes for the non-fashion part of it, you will want enough merchandise to fill forty-five minutes. You might want to show more than one piece per minute (multiples or groups) perhaps sixty to one hundred and twenty pieces. You would then plan on pulling double this number out of stock in order to plan the show.

The amount of merchandise is doubled in the beginning for several reasons. Everything shown must be fitted on a model, accessorized, pressed and generally readied for presentation, and all in advance; it is better to have too much at the beginning and eliminate later than have to go through this process at the last minute. Much of what you pull will automatically be eliminated as you go along. What looks great on a hanger may not wear well. Some clothes look better close up than from a runway. Other items may not be dramatic enough. Color may wash out, or distinctive detailing might be lost. Certain silhouettes may be unflattering. You'll want to edit these out. Also, models and clothes will appear in a certain sequence and you'll want to group clothes for their effect and line up models to allow them enough time to change. With more merchandise than you need, you give yourself the flexibility to coordinate both—to shift around to accommodate every aspect.

A short show, such as a children's show (knowing the limited attention span of children in the audience) might run a half hour with a quick introduction and close. Thirty to sixty pieces might be shown, pulling sixty to one hundred and twenty pieces on the outset.

Making a Blueprint for the Merchandise

Show planning moves from the general to the particular. Once the general theme is decided, a master plan or blueprint is made up showing fashion categories to be included. Specific looks are included within these categories and then individual garments are pulled that reflect each corresponding item listed in the blueprint.

As soon as the basic direction or theme is determined, an *Ideal Chart* is made up and filled in. This is the blueprint that will be followed when pulling merchandise from stock. (See page 44.)

Since the Ideal Chart shows each piece to be pulled, it includes double the number to be shown. It shows what general categories will be covered, making sure that no area is overlooked. A grid is made with separate blank boxes headlined by the various categories to be shown. A seasonal show would have these six basics: sportswear, coats, suits, dresses, evening wear and children's wear. Each heading will have a number to indicate the amount of merchandise to be pulled for it. Here's the first point at which the theme and background come into play.

HOW TO PRODUCE A FASHION SHOW

Pulling double the number of pieces needed guarantees that after eliminations are made, the final lineup is as strong as possible.

If the season's news is predominately sportswear, this category will contain the greatest number of pieces; if it is dresses, this will get the greatest emphasis.

Under each of these headings, specific looks that belong to it will be listed. For instance, under dresses, you might show: one-piece, two-piece, flared skirt, long sleeved, belted, empire. Coats might include street and floor lengths, day and evening, full, narrow, double- and single-breasted, wide and narrow sleeved, high collared, wrapped. Sportswear might include skirts, pants, blouses, sweaters, plus some layered looks, vests and more specific examples within these sub-categories. Listings should be as specific as possible. If white pants or red coats are important, they can be specifically listed here.

The Ideal Chart for a children's show might include school clothes, playclothes, dresses, coats and suits. The playclothes category might include short pants, long pants, corduroys, drip-dry fabrics or tough child-proof fabrics, perhaps a group of clothes that expand and grow with the child. If dark plaid polyester cuffed pants or animal print overalls are important, list them as specifically as this.

The chart then can be adapted to any kind of show, merely by substituting the appropriate categories. The fashion sense that is developed through exposure to showings, press reviews and store personnel tells you what to emphasize. And the listings within the categories can be added to as new store merchandise is reviewed.

Planning the Accessories

The same fashion background needed for the selection of garments is required for accessories. In fact, it is possibly even more important, since the accessories can make or break a look. The fashion planner must know what looks are important and, even more critical, how much to accessorize. Overaccessorizing is an error any time, but in a season of simplicity, it's a dead giveaway that there's

PLANNING THE MERCHANDISE: GARMENTS AND ACCESSORIES

an amateur at work. In general, accessories should dramatize or finish a look without overpowering it.

Accessories should be decided on about the same time as the ready-to-wear. Again, the Ideal Chart is the best way to insure coverage for every category. General category headings would include hats, gloves, shoes, handbags, scarfs, jewelry, stockings and socks. Within the handbag category one could list day and evening bags, shoulder and clutch bags, totes, leather, straw. Your overall fashion view would dictate whether each category would include a few token items or a complete range, depending upon its importance. It may be a season for earrings and scarfs, but no necklaces, in which case, the first two categories would get the greatest emphasis. A miscellaneous category can be included as a catchall for any of the seasonal items that surface, such as silk flowers, barrettes, umbrellas, shawls, dickies, ribbons and whatever else happens to be creating interest. The Ideal Chart for accessories can be set up about the same time or shortly after the ready-to-wear chart.

If it's to be a store show, the fashion coordinator or planner can work with the accessories department to make up the chart and pull the merchandise from stock. With accessories covering such a broad range, it's an asset to work with people who are familiar with the complete store stock on a day-to-day basis. If the accessories staff is unavailable, or if it's a non-retail show, several trips through the various departments covered will help familiarize you with the merchandise.

It is important to coordinate the accessories to the ready-to-wear. Not only will items be pulled out of store stocks that are listed in the chart, but once ready-to-wear is pulled, all accessories areas should be reviewed with an eye toward specific garments. The chart guarantees that all important looks are covered. However, certain ready-to-wear looks may demand some unique piece of jewelry or item that is not listed and is perhaps a "classic" and wouldn't normally appear on the chart or be pulled against it.

Once the two charts are filled in, one can begin the physical process of pulling ready-to-wear and accessories from the stock room and the floor itself. The pulling begins shortly after the planning meeting. It will take several weeks to pull, fit the clothes on the models, alter, press and decide the sequence of clothes; therefore the pulling should begin at least four weeks prior to the show date, and earlier if possible. The procedure must be completed in time for a dress rehearsal and for the program, if one is to be printed.

As you become more adept at planning, fittings can be set up closer to the show date, and much later if no program is used. Keep in mind that pulled garments cannot be sold, so the later they are pulled, the more opportunity for sales.

When beginning to pull the garments, check with buyers to find out how much new stock is in and how much is yet to come. Make sure that the newly ordered merchandise has been shipped in time to make show selections. If ordered merchandise has not been delivered, pull the required number of pieces to cover

HOW TO PRODUCE A FASHION SHOW

the show, new arrivals can be pulled later and substituted, but coordinate the timing with the buyers, so that this is kept to a minimum.

A room should be available to accommodate the merchandise being pulled—preferably a central location near the fashion department. All ready-to-wear and accessories should be assembled here.

Inventory sheets should be made up as the merchandise is taken out of stock. These show where the merchandise was taken from, the purpose, by whom and usually signed by the department manager or buyer. When the merchandise is returned after the show, it will be signed back into the department. The inventory sheets are important because the store can keep track of merchandise being moved around. Despite the extra paper work it guarantees that the merchandise will be returned to its proper department and helps keep down loss and misplacement. Ready-to-wear as it is assembled can be hung on racks which makes it easier to shuffle garments around into groups to see the total effect for the show.

Accessories can be assembled on a table and as they are matched to their garments, can go into bags and hung with the garment on the same racks. In addition to accessories listed on the chart, a quantity should be stockpiled for last minute fill-ins or in case a garment is replaced.

As the garments and accessories are lined up the first round of cuts can be made. Eliminations are usually done by the fashion staff, working as a committee. The first to be eliminated will be garments that look like they will not show to advantage from the runway. The next items to go will be the duplications.

Hang tags and cards can be made up as the racks fill. Both will show a description of the garment and accessories and will list model's names. These models will be fitted into the garments. Several model's names should be listed with each garment. If more than one model is capable of wearing one garment, the sequence of the garments is flexible, with many combinations possible.

The hang tags serve as preliminary identifications of ready-to-wear and accessories and as models come in to be fitted, they can find their clothes quickly on the racks.

Assuming the garment is kept in the show, the cards that have been made up will eventually be filled in further and turned over to the commentator or whoever is writing the script or commentary. As the various categories of clothes begin to take shape and fill out, a sequence number can be assigned.

Shoes are not pulled until later. This saves pulling shoes in several sizes for each model and garment listed. As models are selected and finalized for each garment, the shoes are pulled, taped, identified and stored in boxes near the racks. Extra shoes in basic colors and styles are also assembled in case of last minute replacements. Foundations and necessary lingerie can also be pulled as the final garments are selected.

Once the pulling and identification process is completed, the next step is to bring the models in for fittings.

The Fitting, Run-Off and Rehearsal | 6

The fitting has been aptly described as "marrying the bodies to the merchandise." Literally, models and show garments are teamed for the best possible match. It is more economical in terms of time and money to schedule as few fittings as possible, since it requires booking models and paying for their time as well as having the fashion staff on hand. However, for a show containing eighty or more pieces, three, four or more fittings may be needed with several models booked for each one. On the other hand, informal shows might require quick fittings on a non-scheduled basis. Good professional models have a sixth sense for what they can show well and how to accessorize each look. Fittings should be arranged ten days to two weeks prior to the show. This allows time for alterations and finalizing the selection of clothes before the information is sent to the printer for the program.

To avoid delays during fittings, assemble all equipment needed in advance (See Fitting Room Check List, page 50). Each model will wear between six and eight outfits, depending on her expertise, the length of time needed between changes and the complexity of each change. (Bridal wear is very time-consuming; consequently a model might be able to wear only four pieces.) The pace of the show and the budget for the models should be factored in as well. Models will be fitted into several extra outfits over and above the ones they'll actually wear. This is done to maintain flexibility in planning the show's sequence. One can shuffle garments around without the risk of ending up with the same model showing two garments in a row with no time allowed for her to change.

In addition to the models, the fitting personnel includes fitters or seamstresses, fashion staff and store buyers. During the fitting, the fashion staff makes sure that each garment is assigned to the best possible model. It must not only be flattering, it must fit properly with a minimum of alterations. This keeps the alterations department from having too heavy a workload and keeps alteration charges from getting out of hand. A general idea of costs should be known and budgeted in

Fitting the Clothes

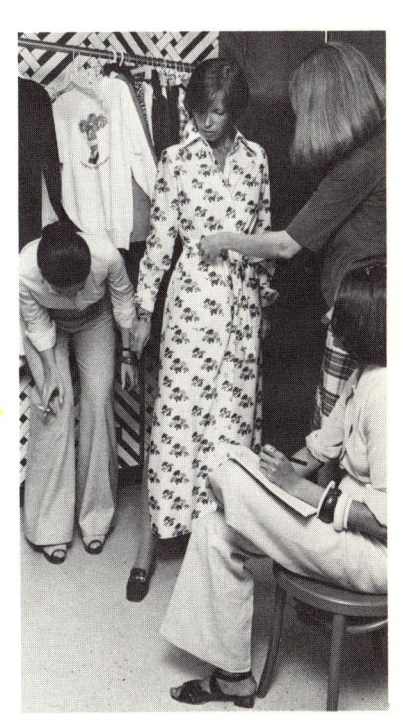

As models are fitted, descriptions and instructions can be noted on cards or sheets, depending on the information system employed.

49

HOW TO PRODUCE A FASHION SHOW

advance (based on prior shows). Most retail shows will utilize the store alterations department. Independent shows can use the services of the store supplying the clothes or a local seamstress, and rough estimates should be requested in advance. Another reason to limit alterations is that the garments may be put back into stock and sold after the show. The fashion staff should include enough people to note who will wear each garment, and to make up cards and sheets for future use. Buyers should be available to check the fit of the garments they have bought, and if they are unable to attend, they should be alerted to a badly cut garment, or one that doesn't fit any of the models.

Garment Tags

The materials listed on the Fitting Room Check List (left) should be assembled prior to fittings to avoid costly delays. A Fitting Sheet (center) can be reproduced in quantity and used to note alterations, props and as model sheets. Although the information on the Model Sheet (right) can be consolidated with that on the Fitting Sheet, it has two advantages which could be important to a large show: 1) each model can post her single sheet in her assigned area and 2) the staff can organize her area from a single sheet.

Several members of the staff should be present during a fitting since cataloguing information is time-consuming and complicated. As each garment is assigned to a model and altered to fit, it is properly tagged (or if already tagged during the pulling, then the model's name is simply added). At this stage, every tag should contain the model's name, a brief description of the garment and a category number. Constantly referring to the Ideal Chart will insure that each category is fully represented. Either during the pulling and assembling of the merchandise or at the fitting, each category can be assigned a number or letter. Garment tags can then show the particular category to which the merchandise belongs.

Fitting Room Check List

Furniture should include tables, chairs, platform (if a runway will be used), enough clothing racks to hold garments comfortably (garments will be shifted as the run-off is worked out; extra space may be needed to separate garments returned from alterations or for "rejects").

Supplies:

Fitting Sheets
Model Sheets
cards for commentary
garment tags
pens, pencils
staplers
straight and safety pins
scissors
tailors chalk
measuring tape
cellophane tape
tape for shoes
shopping bags
hangers
dress shields
scarfs to protect models' hair & makeup
accessories for each garment (shoes, belts, etc. that affect a look or proportion)
foundations for each garment (those that can affect garment fit)

Fitting Sheet

Name _____ No. _____

Shoe _____ Hosiery _____ Head _____

Description:

Accessories:

hat
belt
shoes
hosiery
handbag
gloves
foundations
scarf
jewelry
other

Model Sheet

Name _____

Ht. _____ Head _____

Shoe _____ Hosiery _____

No. _____

Description:

Accessories:

Props:

Makeup/Hair:

Note:

No. _____

Description:

Accessories:

Props:

Makeup/Hair:

Note:

50

THE FITTING, RUN-OFF AND REHEARSAL

In addition to the garment tags, fitting or garment sheets can be made up for each piece. Each of these lists the model's name (or names, if the model has not been determined), category number (and sequence number, if known), a complete description of the garment and accessories. Once the model is determined, her shoe, head and other sizes can be added. The fitting sheets can be the basis of a very efficient information system. Coupled with the garment tags no other cataloguing is necessary. Several copies of these sheets can be made up and used in dressing rooms to line up the models, to send to the copy department, commentator or to whomever writes the commentary. They can be shuffled around to try various combinations and sequences of clothes. A single notebook of fitting sheets can be annotated to serve as a running check list of what alterations and accessorizing have yet to be completed.

Fitting Sheets

An alternate information system to the fitting sheets calls for both commentary cards and model sheets. The commentary cards should contain the model's name, a fuller description of the garment and the accessories when they are added, as well as the category number. A major advantage to filling out the commentary cards during the fitting, aside from speed, is that subtleties of fit that might not be noticed about a garment on the rack will stand out on the model. For instance, a bloused waist, hem length, dropped or elongated shoulder will be readily seen and noted. Descriptive information on these cards should include any selling points such as type of fabric, ease of care or lack of seasonality.

Commentary Cards

The model sheets contain the model's name, height, shoe, stocking and foundation sizes. Eventually each garment and its accessories will be listed in order. However, until the sequence of clothes is finalized just the model's name and statistics, category number, and number of pieces each is to wear will suffice. Category numbers should be checked continuously to make sure that each model's changes are evenly distributed over the various groupings.

Model Sheets

At the same time, the type of foundations needed for each garment should be noted. This information can be added to the tags and should definitely be noted on the fitting sheets and model sheets, although it is not necessary for the commentary cards.

There is another process going on continuously during both the pulling and the fittings. The merchandise is constantly being edited by the fashion staff to include only the best and most dramatic examples of each fashion point and category covered.

Once the fittings are completed, the run-off or sequence of garments can be finalized. This becomes a fairly easy task working with the tagged garments on the racks. The simplest way to structure the run-off is around the Ideal Chart.

The Run-Off

HOW TO PRODUCE A FASHION SHOW

Above: The technique of grouping similar styles is used to emphasize a point about tops. Left: Kenzo's Prêt-à-Porter show. (Courtesy of Women's Wear Daily.*) Right: "The Big Number," featuring editorial looks for* Seventeen *Magazine, presented by Jordan Marsh, Boston.*

The categories can be maintained for the major groups in the show, starting with sportswear and building to the more dramatic evening looks.

One of the basic methods for building the merchandise sequence is grouping. This is the technique of putting similar looks together and showing them consecutively or simultaneously to make a strong, clear point and to demonstrate a fashion message. Impact is achieved through repetition.

Structuring the sequence according to the Ideal Chart categories is one example of grouping. This way the sportswear message as well as day dresses, evening clothes, coats, etc., is defined and refined. Within these basic categories, it is possible to further group. If an important point is color, a grouping of two or more items can be put together; plaids or prints can be put together for the same reason. A group of separates, certain jacket styles, or short evening dresses can be shown at one time. The technique is flexible allowing for large or small groupings. In fact, clothes can be grouped throughout the show to demonstrate major points. For instance, the mix and match or layering concepts can be illustrated throughout the show in several categories, i.e., sportswear, dresses,

THE FITTING, RUN-OFF AND REHEARSAL

evening wear. "How to" shows, where strong points need emphasis, lend themselves to groupings, i.e., several simple dresses, accessorized up or down; the same dress on several figure types to demonstrate the fine art of camouflage.

The purpose of a finale is to wind the show up on a single, bold and exciting note —to leave the audience gasping and clapping. The finale is the last impression the audience will have so it should be strong and well-coordinated.

The Finale

The easiest finale to set up is to bring all the models back on stage in their final numbers and have them pivot on cue and exit. The numbers alone guarantee a certain impact. This can be heightened further by ending with evening looks or luxurious at-home wear and parading them as the finale. While no new elements have been added, it is dramatic, recalls the ambience of the show, and cues the audience to show their enjoyment and appreciation. This type of finale can be accomplished in several ways, the pieces can be brought out all at once and commentated individually in detail, or with just a remark about where they can be found. They can also be shown individually, having models remain on stage, or return at the end for a final pivot. A traditional ending for a seasonal show uses bridal gowns to achieve the bold effect—either a group of them or a tableau, with bride, groom, maids, flower girl and ring bearer.

Even a fashion parade might employ the tactics of a spectacular for a finale. This could include a special backdrop, props, extra models, special lighting effects. The bridal finale could be executed using a stained glass window to suggest a church, with the wedding party parading the runway in pairs, the bride and groom exiting through a hail of rice. Evening wear could be introduced in a ballroom with dancing couples departing down the runway as their garments are described. The basic principle common to all shows is to save the best and most dramatic for last.

Once the order of categories and the fashions within these categories are determined by moving them around on the racks, the next step in laying out the sequence of show garments is to work out a final run-off. At this point, the approximate number of pieces to be shown is established, as well as the total amount of time to be devoted to the fashion portion of the show. Adding to this the rule of thumb to show at least one piece per minute (several times that where groups are used), a close ratio can be worked out between pieces and allotted time.

If there are more pieces than the timing allows, the conflict can be resolved in several ways. The fashions can be further edited; groupings can be added and more multiples shown; the pace can be adjusted by planning to show two or three garments simultaneously throughout the show. Editing and grouping give the run-off flexibility. It is possible to vary the pace by dividing the categories or groupings and showing some parts consecutively, some two at a time, and others in groups of five or six simultaneously. Obviously this kind of varied pacing makes the show much more interesting.

The garment tag can include names of all models who have been fitted; all but the final choice can be crossed out. The sequence number can be added later. "F" means the garment has been fitted; "A" that it has been altered and returned (a simple way of coordinating the garment "traffic"). The reverse side might include alteration instructions and/or accessories.

HOW TO PRODUCE A FASHION SHOW

A simple and dramatic finale can be staged by having all models return to the stage in their final numbers. (Courtesy of Hutzler's, Maryland and Glamour *Magazine.)*

The final sequence therefore should be a combination of these techniques, and rarely is it finalized in one stroke. The editing and grouping process is a matter of polishing and refining that takes place over a period of time—from the first pulling through the dress rehearsal.

Coordinating Models and Merchandise

A week to ten days prior to the show, the run-off should be finalized. This allows time to have programs printed and to schedule rehearsals. The final weeding out of garments should take place now. In proper order all garments, tagged and with alterations completed, bags identified by category number and model's name containing corresponding accessories, should be on clothes racks. With the run-off definite, it is now possible to assemble and coordinate models and merchandise. All hang tags should be removed from clothes and accessories. All shoes should be taped. In addition to accessories, each shopping bag should contain the proper foundations.

At this point, the model sheets can be completed. These list in proper order

THE FITTING, RUN-OFF AND REHEARSAL

the pieces to be shown by each model. All accessories and foundations are included. The sheet is displayed prominently in the changing area set aside for each model and will be referred to by her and her dresser. If the fitting sheet system is employed, a clipboard arrangement for the sheets can be used in lieu of the single model sheet.

At this stage, all show merchandise should be ready for a dress rehearsal. Garments should be altered, pressed and hung on racks with attached bags of accessories. Any accessories too large for the bags, such as hats, boots or props should be boxed or bagged separately and identified with numbers corresponding to the garments.

A good size collection of accessories and foundations to be used for emergencies should be assembled in the same area. These can also be bagged and clearly identified as well, along with a large trunk or box containing basic equipment for the model room. The final step will be to move the merchandise and equipment into the dressing room. It can go "as is" if the trip is a short one, across the store. If trucking is involved, plastic covers or dust sheets are often sufficient protection. Racks can be covered and transported intact. Pressing irons, hair curlers, makeup and other dressing room equipment will be shipped along with the clothes.

The term run-through, specifically refers to the rehearsal of the show sequence. Rehearsal is a term used interchangeably but one that has a broader application, referring also to the advance training of models and practicing of show numbers. The number of rehearsals and run-throughs scheduled will be determined by the complexity of the show and the skill of the models.

Rehearsal and Run-Through

A dress rehearsal is a minimum requirement even for a simple show and well-seasoned models. It is common practice to schedule a complete run-through of the show in addition to the dress rehearsal. This means booking models and alerting the fashion staff in advance. At the preliminary run-through the route the models will take should be paced out and timed, including entrances, exits and pivots. In laying out the route, the number of show pieces and the design of the stage and runway must be taken into consideration. Most professional models can pick up the route, entrances and exits, and turns simply by explaining them and running through it once or twice to make sure it's workable. When choreography or amateur models are involved, demonstration, instruction and separate rehearsals are needed. All models should be checked for correct carriage and pace as well as the ability to walk and pivot properly—this, in addition to knowing how to show ensembles, jackets or coats. Amateurs can be taught these techniques at separate rehearsals. Professionals who don't know the basics should be eliminated from future shows since one is paying for their expertise.

Once models are familiar with the run-off and route, a final run-through or dress rehearsal can be arranged. This is usually done the same day as the show with time allowed before the actual show for everyone to relax and reorganize.

HOW TO PRODUCE A FASHION SHOW

Above: Sequence is finalized on racks. Shopping bags contain accessories and foundations. Right: Clothes and accessories are returned to racks and bags ready to be returned to stock or shipped to another show.

56

THE FITTING, RUN-OFF AND REHEARSAL

Sometimes these rehearsals are scheduled at a time when store personnel can attend. This serves as valuable sales training—familiarizing the whole selling staff with current fashion merchandise and the philosophy behind it.

The dress rehearsal is the final assembly of the show elements before the show. It should be executed exactly as the show.

During the dress rehearsal, all personnel involved in any way with the show should be on hand and at their respective posts. This includes the complete dressing room staff as well as the fashion staff, the commentator, the introductory speaker and the lighting technicians. (In fact, the only personnel excluded should be musicians for budgetary reasons and the florist, if one is used.) The segments are assembled and timed: opening remarks, fashion portion, closing comments, credits and the lead-in to the intermission or giveaways if these are part of the show. The dress rehearsal, like the run-through, is timed with a stopwatch. The music and lighting are cued for each section. If the fashion part is ragged or slow, the source of the problem should be identified quickly and corrected with a minimum of change in the sequence—often it is the dressers or starter who by holding back models are unwittingly causing the delay. Sometimes, the slowness can be corrected by editing introductory remarks. The total time lapse should correspond closely to the advance plan. It is important to alert staff to changes made at this point, and vital that they are recorded on all model or fitting sheets. With tension and nerves a natural part of last minute preparations, a staff member should be assigned the specific responsibility of seeing that all changes are noted.

Final cues should be given to models and coordinated with the commentator. A guest commentator who arrives after directions are given to models may want to set up a cue system that can supersede previous instruction during the show. Most experienced commentators have a good sense of timing and an instinct for the audience. Armed with a simple set of cues to bring the next model on stage, or send her off the runway, the commentator can control the pace better and smooth out areas that appear to be unevenly paced. At the same time the staff member assigned to sending out the models (see *Starter*, page 89) can serve to check or speed up the pace as well.

After the dress rehearsal, the clothes and accessories are returned to their proper places in the dressing room. Each item should be examined to make sure it hasn't been damaged or wrinkled.

Packing Up the Show

After the show is over, merchandise will either be returned to stock or transported to a new site for another show. In either case, speed and organization are essential. Since the longer it is out of stock, the less chance the merchandise has of being sold, it should be back in the various departments by the next day. This means carefully checking through the inventory sheets to determine the proper department, retagging garments and accessories, and checking them off these sheets.

HOW TO PRODUCE A FASHION SHOW

Buyers or department managers must be alerted when an item is missing or damaged enough to be marked down.

When clothes will be on display after the show, they should be returned to a central point where they can be seen at close hand and tried on. Arrangements can be made to clear a special area in the store for this. Clothes can be left on racks, but accessories and bags should be removed for security reasons. Clothes should never be displayed in the dressing room itself—there is too much equipment and small gear that could be broken or removed. For co-op or non-store shows, it is easier and safer to tell the audience where the merchandise can be found at a later date.

Security precautions should be observed during the packing up process and until the clothes are returned to stock or loaded onto trucks. During this period of confusion after the show, the dressing room area is particularly vulnerable to theft. Large hotels especially attract people who make a career out of this kind of theft.

The dressing room, if it is a temporary one on the selling floor, should also be dismantled as quickly as possible. This precludes loss and keeps disruption of normal store selling activities and traffic to a minimum.

Models—
Choosing, Training and Evaluating Them | 7

By definition, a model is "one who is employed to display clothes or other merchandise." A model is also "an example for imitation or emulation." If these criteria were always observed, many headaches could be avoided. Professional models are preferable to work with for a number of reasons, however from time to time, circumstances will dictate the use of amateurs. There are certain specifications, physical and attitudinal, to be met in a model, whether professional or amateur.

One of the most important qualifications, of course, is size. Since clothes should be altered minimally, models should be a standard size and well-proportioned. The ideal misses sizes would be 8, 10 (preferable), or 12 and 5' 4" to 5' 7" tall. Junior sized models should be 7 or 9 (preferable) and 5' 4" to 5' 7" tall. In women's clothes size 14 is best, although size 16 is acceptable. Children's sizes vary greatly depending on the age group. Child models could be virtually any size, as long as they're standard sizes and attractively proportioned.

Models should be attractive and distinctive looking without necessarily being beautiful. Vitality, personality, or any other quality an audience can enjoy and identify with should be looked for in choosing models. All models should be able to walk well and move gracefully.

Equally important is a professional attitude. Anyone earning a living as a model will take it seriously, observing booking times and willing to wear whatever merchandise is selected. A good amateur will have the same attitude.

Other qualities are important. An ability to show clothes to their best advantage with practiced ease (or the ability to learn the basics quickly). An instinct that tells a model what selling points to emphasize. A love of fashion and a flair for wearing clothes with distinction. An understanding of proportion and an ability to accessorize clothes if called on to do so. A respect for the clothes being shown. A friendly and cooperative attitude toward co-workers. An ability to be her own makeup artist and hair stylist if necessary. And certainly, responsiveness

Model Requirements

Vitality on the runway and reliability are hallmarks of a good model—professional or amateur.

HOW TO PRODUCE A FASHION SHOW

to instruction. Given the number of minor mishaps that occur even during a well-run show, and the near chaos of the dressing room during show time, a model should be able to work well under pressure.

Professionals vs. Amateurs

Models fall into two classifications: professional and amateur. Professional models can be photographic or runway models. Most photographic models are also adept at runway showing. Experienced runway models are easier by far to work with than amateurs. Through experience, most have developed a sixth sense for showing clothes properly, are quick to pick up directions and cues, responsible about appointments, careful with clothes and maintain their aplomb in the face of small catastrophies.

A model's performance can enhance or destroy months of careful preparation. Many amateurs do take their modeling assignments as seriously as professionals, but the difference may lie in the degree of commitment. And the threat of problems because of this can cause nightmares for a show coordinator. When coordinators get together and trade stories of mishaps, the odds are they involved amateur models. Anecdotes about models who fly down the runway like bats or faint at the entrance are amusing years later, but during the show havoc is wrought.

There should always be a good reason for using an amateur model. Since the responsibility for the quality of the show lies with the coordinator, regardless of whether professionals or amateurs are used, the extra training and work should be weighed against the advantages of amateurs. One advantage is the savings in model fees. Sometimes the cost factor is a major one because of increases in labor, hotel and equipment charges. In fact, many retailers today are using amateurs almost exclusively for this reason. (You can also hire one or two professionals and use them to train the amateurs.) Another advantage is their drawing power. Audiences love to see friends and relatives, so if amateurs substantially increase attendance or make a significant contribution to the audience's enjoyment, they are worth using. However, before making a commitment to use an amateur, it is vital that she be aware of exactly what the job entails—that it can be tedious as well as exciting, gruelling as well as glamorous, that it demands her attention and physical presence at specified times and that the organization has invested thousands of dollars towards the success of the show, in order to make a profit or raise funds, and is relying on her.

Another type of model that is used on occasion is the performer, most often actors or dancers. They are used when the presentation of the show is dependent on professionally choreographed (and professionally executed) dance routines. This will occur rarely, since most runway models can pick up the simple routines or disco steps with a few rehearsals. Dancers have the advantage of litheness and ability—sometimes however, their physical development is extremely noticeable and detracts from the clothes.

A dance sequence is used to show the movement and sensuality of the fabrics at an intimate apparel showing. (Courtesy of Celanese Corporation.)

MODELS—CHOOSING, TRAINING AND EVALUATING THEM

Among both amateurs and professionals, certain models have qualities that suit them to specific types of shows.

CHILDREN—Amateur and professional child models are obviously best for children's wear shows or for appearances in seasonal or other shows. Professionals have three distinct advantages over amateurs: (1) they have the experience of being in front of large groups of people and are less likely to become upset; (2) they are used to working with strangers; (3) their mothers know how to be available and yet stay out of the way. Child models should be well supervised. In addition to individual dressers, a starter should be provided who understands children. It is also wise to station someone near the foot of the runway in case trouble develops there, a long way from help. Children are a wonderful drawing card and by and large, the audience is sympathetic and understanding when something occurs that isn't in the script.

TEENAGERS—Most teens are extremely eager to model. Predominately amateurs, the overwhelming advantages are their eagerness, which enables them to respond well to instructions, and their vitality, which comes across on the runway. This same vitality once in a while results in excitement and noise backstage, but on the whole, their freshness is a plus for the junior shows and a great source of enjoyment to the audience.

SOCIETY WOMEN—There's no better way to guarantee a good turnout at a charity benefit than by using socially prominent local women. They are also the most demanding group to work with. They have a tendency to break or be late for appointments; they are decided in their opinions of what garments suit them. Also, in order to guarantee a good turnout, it is important to select the leaders among them—the ones whom others will follow. These women in effect "underwrite" the show by lending their prestige. Since these leaders are not always model sizes, it requires tremendous tact to choose the most attractive and avoid the ones with problem figures—and expect them to turn out in support of the charity event.

OLDER WOMEN—These women are invariably professionals or experienced amateurs, and are used for the older woman's show, "how to" show, specialty show or as part of a seasonal effort. The success of these women as models depends on their credibility with their special audience. It means finding women who have mature good looks, trim figures and "real" appeal. Too young and too attractive models will inspire an "I-could-never-look-like-that!" reaction that extends to the clothes. A conservative audience must be able to identify with them.

BRIDES—Working with amateurs in this show has great advantages. Bridal wear has great emotional appeal and only very fresh-faced models can carry off the look. An old or jaded face framed in white veiling is a real shock. Brides-to-be

Types of Models

A model should be able (and equipped) to do her own makeup and style her own hair.

HOW TO PRODUCE A FASHION SHOW

culled from the store's clientele make excellent models in terms of looks and audience appeal. Bridal wear is difficult to show and models should be instructed not to attempt anything more than a straight walk down the runway with a pause in the middle or at the end. If the stage area is deep and smooth-surfaced, a wide turn can be attempted, but only with trainless gowns and floor length or shorter veils. If possible, replace any steps on to the runway or platform with a ramp; with a bouquet in one hand, a full skirt is hard to manage and easy to step on.

INFORMAL MODELS—The same basic requirements hold for models at informal showings as for runway shows. An additional quality of friendliness is important, since models should be able to strike up a conversation about the garment or take the initiative and volunteer information if it appears that a customer is interested but hesitant about asking for details. Many stores use attractive sales personnel to model informally and this arrangement seems to work well, as long as they don't use it as an opportunity to "visit" among friends.

MALE MODELS—Men are a welcome addition to a show. However, few men can carry the role off without feeling—and looking—uncomfortable. Using a group of men who are friends to participate in a charity show seems to make the idea at least tolerable to them, but most men balk at the idea of modeling and do it awkwardly and unwillingly. (It has been reported that a glass of champagne can overcome this awkwardness—you can use your own judgment as to that.) The best sources of male models is either an agency or local theater guild, where actors are available who will gladly supplement their income by modeling.

ELA GERARD
MANNEQUIN AGENCY
586 7716

HEIGHT 5'7½"
SIZE 6-7-8
HAIR Dk. Blonde
EYES Hazel
SHOE 8½M.

Models can be selected from head sheets. However, if you'd like to see them in person, you can request a "go-see" through the agency.

Professional Standards

Models, amateur or professional, should be guided by a set of principles—and judged by these same standards in terms of future employment.

1. Punctuality for all appointments.
2. Professional models should honor all bookings on a first come basis, even if a more lucrative offer is available later.
3. All models should arrive at least a half hour prior to the dress rehearsal and show.
4. Models should be equipped with basic items in the way of foundations, makeup and hair care items for their personal use. Minimum foundations should include bra and pants, body stocking and sheer stockings in neutral tones. Unless a makeup artist or cosmetics are provided, models should provide themselves with everything they'll need. Unless a hair stylist is provided, model's equipment should include heated rollers, wigs and hairpieces, brushes, pins, ribbons and whatever is needed to turn themselves out. Hair styles should be kept simple since time is at a premium; one look for day and one for evening is all that is essential. Models should also have a scarf or

MODELS—CHOOSING, TRAINING AND EVALUATING THEM

covering to protect hair and makeup (and clothes) when changing, and dress shields as well.

5. Models should treat garments with respect. Garments should look untouched when they're returned to stock.
6. Models are responsible for learning and following all instructions, for knowing the route and all dance routines.
7. Models should be willing to wear whatever is assigned to them. Some models will not model foundations or sheer lingerie. These questions should be settled in advance.
8. Models should be willing to accessorize their assigned outfits if requested to do so.
9. Models should also remove or replace hang tags on clothes that need it.
10. Models should keep conversation to a minimum during rehearsals and keep voices down so they're not heard by the audience.
11. Models should keep calls to a minimum, and then, only short business calls.

While models fall into basic categories, most models are adaptable and can play the ingenue or femme fatale equally well.

ANITA Brunette 6-8 5'8" 8½M

KATHY Aurre Brunette 6-8 5'8" 8

ELAINE Bedell Blonde 8-10 5'8" 8½B

BRIDGET Benson Dark Brown 6-8 5'9" 9B

CAROL Brandt Blonde 6-8 5'8" 7½B

HOW TO PRODUCE A FASHION SHOW

Sources for Models — Most of the larger cities have agencies that specialize in runway models. A list of these agencies can be culled from the *Yellow Pages* and a phone call or a visit to each will produce head sheets of registered models, file cards with statistics and lists of current clients. From this it will be easy to tell which agencies are best for your particular needs.

Often models, especially when they are getting started, or in the smaller cities, will call or come in for appointments. At least one past employer should be called to weed out possible "no-shows."

For amateurs, there are a number of sources. The store itself is a prime one. Sales personnel make good models if they meet the requirements. (Avoid using fashion staff members except as emergency stand-ins, aside from schedule conflicts, it is too heavy a workload to ask anyone to carry.) Store personnel can recommend customers or local women that might want to model.

Within the store, a teen or college board is a good source for young models. The selling staff in the children's department can solicit models by asking the mothers who shop in the department. And the bridal consultant or registrar usually has a list of current brides-to-be, whether or not they're store customers. Both retailers and independent organizations can also set up tryouts for models. This will also serve as advance publicity for the show as well as assuring a good selection of models to choose from.

For a charity event, society women can be approached either officially through the organization itself or through a mutual friend. If possible, write to the president of the organization giving show information and spelling out requirements as to figure types and time schedules. This will help to avoid the problem of tactfully refusing someone's services later.

In addition to the agencies, a coordinator involved in an independent show can use this last approach—writing several local women's organizations as well as contacting local department stores for models.

Over a period of time, most coordinators develop a group of models they use repeatedly as the core of the show lineup. With this kind of experience, an amateur is as important and valuable as a professional—more so, since she can teach new models the routines developed during past shows.

A professional audience requires professional models. Trade shows of any kind demand professionals since the presentation must be as slick and sophisticated as possible. This kind of audience is not only demanding and critical, it can recognize an amateur immediately.

Booking Models — Standard procedure on booking models varies among agencies. If certain models are in heavy demand, or the show is being held during the peak season (which is usually the case), you may have to book months in advance. Usually two or three weeks is sufficient advance notice—sometimes a few days will do. If exact show dates are unknown, you can make tentative bookings for several alternative dates.

MODELS—CHOOSING, TRAINING AND EVALUATING THEM

RICH'S

Pinwale detailing with cotton corduroy. TOM BOY OF CALIFORNIA gets high marks and blazers the skirt and jackets the pants with equal aplomb in a soft heathery green. Left: the belted 25" skirt $18. Pocketed blazer $24. Design accented acrylic turtleneck in deep brown $10. Challis patchwork print shirt $16. Right: Shirtjacket $22. Straight line pants $17. Cotton knit mitered striped skivvy in multi hues $10

Denise Cummins — Shamrock
Elise Goldwasser — Northside
Tina Graham — Sylvan Hills
Mary Grant — Roswell
Alice Hollahan — Briarcliff
Laurel Hubbard — North Fulton
Lee Maginnis — Clarkston
Janel Murrey — Riverwood

Rich's and Seventeen Roadshow

Seventeen—August 1975

Teen and College Boards are a good source of models. Rich's Atlanta, capitalized on their drawing power in this show ad.

Broadway singers and dancers being fitted for the Deering Milliken Breakfast Show.

But the agency will begin pressuring you to convert them to firm bookings, cancelling the others. So the sooner you can confirm a booking, the better. Make sure in advance, how much grace time you have on tentative bookings and when you would be charged for the time.

When you call to book, give all possible dates for the show or shows, dress rehearsals, other rehearsals and fittings. Find out if there is a minimum time per booking—often it is one hour. Most fittings and rehearsals will not exceed an hour. You will be billed for the half hour prior to the show, when the models are preparing, but not for travel time to or from bookings. You can also book by the day or the job.

Work with amateur models on the same basis. Since you expect the same punctuality from them it is only fair to give them advance notice and firm dates as soon as possible.

Model Fees and Gifts Most model agencies work on an hourly fee basis. When booking many models from the same agency for several hours, investigate the possibility of a flat fee arrangement or a "bulk rate"—that is, the number of hours is totalled and discounted to encourage or reward the store or organization for giving a single

MODELS—CHOOSING, TRAINING AND EVALUATING THEM

agency all its business. If a store has a standing arrangement to use informal models on a day-to-day basis, this should be pointed out during the negotiations.

When using professionals find out whether or not there are any restrictions or rules about publicity photographs. If necessary get a release signed by the models, and if there is a surcharge for any special promotions or any photos in which these models appear, you might want to use amateurs instead. A store can opt to pay amateurs either reasonable compensation for their time or a token fee. This is beneficial in that one can be more exacting when the models are being paid for their services, but may defeat the purpose of using amateurs to keep down expenses. Since everyone works better when a "carrot" of some kind is offered, the store might give gifts rather than money. It could be a small item carried in the store, a gift certificate or an offer of a ten or twenty percent discount on a specified amount of merchandise—which also encourages purchases by models.

With charity shows, it is a graceful gesture for the store to make a donation to the organization in the name of the models in lieu of payments or gifts for their services. Child labor laws, or sometimes parental arrangements, will govern gifts or fees to child models.

If the show is being held outside the store, union rules should be investigated. Particularly when television studios, convention halls, large hotels and theaters are involved. The requirements may affect the choice of models as well as the fees involved.

NAME	AGENCY
ADDRESS	PHONE
HT.	SIZE
SHOES	HEAD
HOSIERY	HAIR
EYES	
REMARKS	

Remarks can include a rating of model's performance such as whether or not she was prompt, cooperative, presented clothes well. Also, miscellaneous information such as whether or not she has a car, is available for travel, will model foundations, lingerie. It is important to include type: mature woman, teen, etc.

Models should be judged against the set of rules outlined earlier in this chapter. Since the coordinator's job becomes harder without complete cooperation from the models, one should be fairly ruthless about eliminating models who do not measure up to standards.

The fashion office should develop a card file on models. This should contain the name, address, telephone number and all pertinent statistics on every model used. Any models who apply in person or through an agency and who seem likely candidates for future use should go into the model file. These cards should be updated after each show, and evaluative remarks can be recorded on the reverse side. They should cover the caliber of each model's performance and also their particular type of look. Simple designations such as "good teen or bride" or "very sophisticated" will make the model selection process easier when future bookings are being arranged. The model file has another application. When model sheets are made up during fittings, the statistics can be transferred from the cards. In addition, when models become familiar, staff members can begin pulling accessories in the proper sizes immediately.

Evaluating Models

Training models falls into two separate areas: (1) teaching routines, routes and cues for a specific show; (2) training inexperienced models in the proper way to show.

Training Models

67

HOW TO PRODUCE A FASHION SHOW

Giving instructions in specific arrangements for a show can be accomplished either through a run-through or if the instructions are not too complicated for more experienced models just before the dress rehearsal. The easiest way is to start at the entrance and pace it off. This includes showing the pace, indicating the spots where pivots and pauses will occur and continuing to the proper exit. If the route varies from appearance to appearance, the changes can be noted on the model sheets hung in the dressing rooms. Another aspect that should be pointed out is the time lapse between each model's entrance. The best way is to identify the spot where the model just ahead will be when the second model should make her appearance. If the first model exits completely, then the next model must be more sensitive to the commentator as she will be totally dependent on voice (or music) cues to guide her on and off the runway.

If several models are to appear in a group and parade consecutively, the order should be firmly established, so that the lead model won't hesitate, even for a second.

If dance steps are called for, you can either demonstrate to the group or teach the steps to one model and let the others pick them up from her. Routines, choreographed by a professional dancer, can be taught during special rehearsals called for that purpose.

When mapping out the route the models will take, include the portion from exit to dressing room. It should be the most direct and quickest. And be sure models and their dressers know precisely how much time they have for each change.

Teaching new models the basics can be time-consuming, but not difficult. The first step is showing them how to walk properly. It used to be a model was trained to a specific posture and walk—easily recognizable because it was so unnatural. Parisian models walked with body bent back, their upper torso following behind the lower half. American models were bent forward, slightly round shouldered. Both walked with long strides and no up-and-down motion whatsoever. Happily, the current look is natural—quick, smooth steps with back straight. Most models are taught to walk straight down the runway and exit.

To slow or vary the pace, pauses and pivots can be added. A back rock is the basis for both. To pause, the model stops with her weight on her forward foot, quickly rocks back onto her back foot, then continues walking forward.

The pivot or turn begins the same way. Rocking back, she then takes a step forward making a half turn on the ball of her back foot just before she shifts her weight to the forward foot. Another back rock, turn and forward step brings her around in a complete turn and she continues. The pace is crisp, with clean half circle turns. Breaking it down into segments of a few movements makes it easier to pick up quickly.

Coats and jackets are unbuttoned from the bottom up; they are slipped off the shoulders, folded and carried over one arm. This is preferable to throwing a jacket

MODELS—CHOOSING, TRAINING AND EVALUATING THEM

Models poised behind backdrop for entry-cue. (Courtesy of The Fashion Group.)

or coat around like a bullfighter's cape or dragging it behind. While these are effective ways to demonstrate throwaway chic, the soiled items are hard to sell at full price.

If it isn't necessary to take off the coat or jacket, the top piece can be slipped off the shoulders to show sleeves and details of the underneath garment. Crooking the arms at the elbows keeps the top piece from sliding down the arms and off.

The other aspect to stress from the very beginning is a smiling face. A friendly smile covers a multitude of gaffes and guarantees a positive audience response.

Commentator and Commentary | 8

As the sophistication level of the consumer has risen, the role of the commentator has become less important. At one time the audience looked to her for even the most basic information—which she provided, right down to the last buttonhole. With the greater awareness of audiences, today's merchandise and its highly graphic presentation, a commentator is sometimes not needed, or used. Many types of shows however, still require a commentary and the degree of importance will vary from show to show. While the commentator's job is diminished, her basic role is still to provide information. This should be primarily generic, conveying the ambience and direction of the current season. The clothes (and accessories) on the runway are the means of demonstrating the specific points being made.

The commentator functions in other ways as well. She—or he—is a merchandiser, a seller of fashion, presenting the information in such a way that it becomes vivid, relevant and appealing. She can be a cohesive force using the commentary and recurring fashion themes to bind the show and its various categories together. And a good commentator becomes a controlling factor, determining the pace and dynamics of the show. She is sensitive enough to the audience to keep the show in synch with its moods, quickening the pace at one point, slowing down for a further explanation at another. And while she's controlling the pace, she must be alert to a hold-up backstage or a first-time model's desire to run instead of walk. She has to compensate for these problems to avoid gaps in the presentation.

The physical requirements are few: she must be attractive and well-groomed to appeal to an audience, and have a good, well-modulated voice. Since she is selling fashion, her overall appearance must reflect her interest in it. Furthermore, she is presenting herself to the store or sponsoring organization and the audience as a fashion expert and her appearance should be a walking advertisement for that expertise. Her makeup, hair, dress and accessories should all be current and put

The Role of the Commentator

A Mademoiselle Magazine commentator during a workshop. Establishing a rapport with the audience helps put the clothes across.

Qualifications

HOW TO PRODUCE A FASHION SHOW

together with flair. A few years ago flair meant a large picture hat and vivid eye shadow. Today, there is no such distinguishing characteristic. In fact, the commentator's look, while being distinctive and current, should not be extreme or she runs the risk of losing her credibility with the audience.

In terms of dress, either the commentator's own clothes or something from the store is acceptable. Street clothes are suitable for a daytime show; a cocktail, dinner or at-home look is right for an evening show. For impact, either black or white is best. However, any bright color or simple print will do as well. The neckline should be fairly simple.

The skills the commentator brings to the job are developed through experience. Her job is to help put the show across to the audience and she employs all her skills toward this end.

Presentation   A basic skill the commentator brings to a show is the ability to control it. She establishes control over the respective show elements by setting up a cue system. The basic timing is already determined by the show coordinator: the total time lapse and the amount of time each model takes to walk the route. This structure is flexible and allows the commentator to speed up or slow down the pace. Once she establishes cues for bringing on or sending off the models, she can control the pace. If she finds the show dragging, she can cue the next model on a few seconds before the preceding one has exited. She can slow down the pace by lengthening her introductions or by interjecting ad libs about the fashion scene in general, the store or the sponsoring organization. If the models are attentive to her comments, she can go into more descriptive detail, which will hold them on the runway longer. Many commentators develop a distinctive style over the course of many shows. Allowing for this, there are still common denominators that make a presentation successful.

Overall, the presentation should convey excitement. It should be controlled however, since the commentator's objective is to sell the fashions, not compete with them for attention. Vitality is an important quality. There's nothing more boring than a deadpan delivery and unfortunately this is a common result of nervous tension. Another quality an audience responds to is warmth. Beginning with a smile involves the audience even before a word is spoken.

Timing and pace are key factors to holding the audience's attention. They are perhaps the most difficult skills to acquire, and are the distinguishing marks of an experienced commentator. These skills come into play in two areas. One is the show itself—what the script and clothes call for at any given moment to create impact. The other area is the audience itself and how it is responding as the show progresses.

In terms of the show requirements, variety is the key. This will occur naturally if the fashion philosophy is given first followed by the illustration—the individual garments on the runway. If the clothes truly demonstrate the general points

COMMENTATOR AND COMMENTARY

The podium should be positioned so that the commentator has a clear view of the models, the audience and the models' entrance.

made, they can be shown quickly, with a minimum of commentary. The whole show can be paced this way.

If separate or unrelated (but generic) points are being made about each item as it appears, the comments will be more evenly distributed and the pace will be slower. This is less varied—less interesting—and should be confined to small segments within the whole presentation.

Gearing the remarks and pace to the audience while the show is in progress demands more from the commentator. Working in front of many kinds of audiences gives a commentator an instinctive kind of sensitivity to each group. Sometimes there are obvious clues such as restlessness, coughing, talking, signs of losing the audience—or the laughing and clapping that indicates a positive response. Sometimes it is just the sixth sense of the commentator that tells her the audience is right with her, or becoming bored. In the beginning a commentator will be preoccupied with controlling her own nervousness while maintaining control of the show. As it becomes easier to control her nervousness and as she develops confidence, her sensitivity to the audience will become more acute.

Spontaneity is another big plus. With more exposure to an audience, spontaneous ad libs and comments come easily. For the novice it's best to go over all material including ad libs, or fillers, until it's very familiar. An unrehearsed quality is the ideal, but in the beginning, it is safer to know in advance exactly what is going to follow. To develop confidence in one's ability to ad-lib, take a written ad lib cue card and deliver the comment in a different form, rephrasing it at the podium. Once you are comfortable with the spontaneous comment, your mind will keep you supplied with ideas that are filed away during the show preparation. Spontaneous comments are very effective with most shows, bringing you and the audience closer together, because the communication appears to be direct. The obvious exception to this is the scripted show, when the commentary is written out and model, music and lighting are cued into it. An off-the-cuff comment here could have dire consequences.

A sense of humor is another asset, but it isn't mandatory. Most commentators, even old pros, steer clear of jokes and one liners unless they've perfected a good delivery and have tested out the reaction so that they know the lines are genuinely funny. Jokes tend to fall flat; either they're bad or badly delivered, and the ensuing embarrassment leaves the audience squirming in their seats. Commentators generally confine themselves to a comment that brings a smile rather than a laugh —and leave the jokes to the comedians.

Tips and Tricks   Good commentators are made, not born. The best thing a novice can do is practice. Take every opportunity to stand in front of an audience. If you can commentate sales training shows for store personnel, do so. Conduct visitors on tours. Volunteer for lectures and demonstrations. Work with smaller groups of people, building up to a larger audience. Half the battle in the beginning is learning to live with the nerves before the show; the other half is knowing you will perform creditably despite them. Practice speaking as well—both over a public address system and a tape recorder. (The first time you hear your own voice filling a convention hall is disconcerting.) You'll need to learn how far away to hold a microphone so that it picks up your voice and not your breathing; how to modulate your voice so that it's smooth and even. Nerves can make it breathy and high-pitched, so learn to compensate.

Prepare for hold-ups and other disasters as if they were an inevitable part of the show. In the event of a catastrophe, you can smooth over the gaps with fillers. Never go to the podium without a few cards containing fillers. These could be announcements or credits regarding the show or a few generic fashion points. Keep them separate so they can be shuffled around at will. And keep them short; there's nothing worse than launching into a long story only to have the next model appear.

If you position yourself properly at the podium, you should be able to see whether or not the next model is ready. If you get a cue from the starter or someone acting as liaison to the dressing room to stretch out the patter, then carry on with your prepared remarks. This way, the audience never knows there is a problem. If you flag a hold-up with a comment such as, "Well, I guess our model isn't ready yet" the audience is uncomfortable and you've created the impression they are watching an amateur hour.

The biggest test of one's aplomb occurs when a model appears out of order. If the proper card can't be located immediately, the best way to handle it is to ad-lib a quick description or use a pertinent comment on a generic point from the fillers. As with a hold-up, do not call it to the audience's attention by commenting on it.

Before the dress rehearsals, check both the podium and public address system. The podium is essential for several reasons. It's difficult to hold a microphone and shuffle commentary cards at the same time, particularly if the fillers are in a separate pile. It has psychological value as well; it's easier to speak from behind a podium and a good place to rest your hands. Also, you can supply yourself with a glass of water in case your throat goes dry. If possible, place the podium in a position that gives you the clearest view of the entryway so that you can see when the models are ready and waiting.

Test the public address system. Many of them seem to have personalities of their own—often perverse. If you can, have someone familiar with the system stationed near the controls during the show. If not, try to learn whether or not the system has quirks. One of the most common problems is feedback—a loud squawking or buzzing. Most times it can be cured by keeping the microphone and speaker farther apart. Before you approach it, know how to adjust the volume (if it's a small system) and how to turn it on and off. If the microphone has to be raised or lowered to accommodate another speaker, ask him to adjust it before leaving the podium. This will avoid having to put down your cards and adjust it before you can say anything.

If you are prone to nerves, there are a few things you can do to make things a little easier. First of all, before the show steer clear of anyone in it. If a last minute problem develops and if you can do something to help, then get involved —it will take your mind off your own nerves and focus your attention outwards. If you can't do anything to help, move away from the situation.

Since the first two or three minutes are always the most difficult, you can arm yourself with a set speech. Memorize it thoroughly, but keep your cards with you. As soon as you begin to speak, pick out a few people around the room and concentrate on getting your message across to them.

Types and Sources of Commentators

The commentator can be an asset to the show over and above the job she does on the runway. Celebrities, personalities, fashion experts from a publication or manufacturer not only draw a larger audience, they can help publicize the show. In addition, they lend a certain prestige to the group underwriting the show. A fashion coordinator or a local independent commentator has the advantage of knowing a great deal about fashion and how to present it to the audience (whom they know and work with year-round) and the coordinator is available without a fee or without making special arrangements. Who should commentate the show then is a question of weighing the advantages of each against the commitments, fees, etc.

THE FASHION COORDINATOR—For a store show, the most obvious choice is the fashion coordinator. She knows fashion, is familiar with the clothes and knows what would appeal to the audience. For the same reasons she would also be a good choice for an independent charity or co-op show.

THE FREE-LANCE COMMENTATOR—If for some reason the fashion coordinator doesn't seem to be a good choice, most towns have one or more independent or free-lance commentators that could be called on to commentate a show. If a charity is using a fashion consultant she would be a good candidate, as would someone from a public relations or publicity firm specializing in or familiar with fashion.

MAGAZINE COMMENTATORS—Many magazines have staff members who travel throughout the country commentating shows. The advantages in using them are that they are (usually) very experienced, knowledgeable, plus they have good promotional value. It is easier to get advance publicity for the show in the local press with a magazine commentator. Also you can use their merchandising facilities in terms of getting copy and theme ideas as well as using them for promotional tie-ins.

However, there are two possible disadvantages to working with publications. One is that they invariably require advertising or promotional commitments in lieu of a fee and covering expenses for the speaker. Tying in with editorial or advertising merchandise is an advantage, however, sometimes buyers object to covering merchandise commitments involved and the advertising department objects because of the budget.

The other possible problem is which speaker is sent. Magazines have a set number of people who travel to shows. The most experienced are assigned to the stores that advertise heavily in the publication, use their services consistently or stage very large and well-publicized shows. Occasionally a retailer will be sent a commentator with little or no experience. Or the wrong type—a young girl for a mature woman's show or a chic "grande dame" for a teen show. For the most part, these tie-ins are very effective. Working closely with the publication ensures a good commentator and commitments that can be lived with and exploited.

MANUFACTURER'S REPRESENTATIVES—Many apparel manufacturers offer the designer or a promotion or publicity person to commentate. They yield several of the same advantages as the magazine representatives. It is easy to arrange interviews with the designer and the local press for advance publicity for the show. Certainly anyone from the firm would be a plus in terms of fashion knowledge and audience appeal. Occasionally the manufacturer will pay a certain

COMMENTATOR AND COMMENTARY

percentage of the advertising money to promote the show. However this arrangement has its limitations: often a commentator is available only for the manufacturer's own shows—trunk shows or shows that concentrate heavily on their own apparel.

CELEBRITIES AND PERSONALITIES—Both celebrities and personalities (local and national) offer tremendous publicity value. While they may know very little of fashion, their drawing power and promotability offset this completely. And the problem is easy to get around, since they can be supplied with a script or printed cards (and most are used to working that way). There are two possible disadvantages in working with either group (this applies to some designers as well). First is the possibility of "temperament" causing clashes with staff, lateness or prompting them to make unreasonable demands. Unless these are carried to absurd lengths, their egos are well worth pampering in view of their value to the show. The other potential problem would be a conflict of schedule that could cause a cancellation due to another commitment—if they're doing the show without a fee, this is understandable. A different commentator could fill in at the last minute if this occurs, but the audience will undoubtedly be disappointed. If possible, get a guarantee or a contract with the individual or his agent. One way to guarantee an appearance is to heavily publicize the commentator and arrange for as many interviews as possible—it is more difficult to bow out after this kind of exposure.

Arrangements with Commentators

If the commentator is the show coordinator or fashion director, no special arrangements are necessary. However, even if the show is part of her job, someone on staff or a member of store management might want to recognize her efforts with a token gift or flowers.

An independent commentator can be booked as one would a model. The agreement should cover the dress rehearsal, show time and whatever time is needed to become familiar with the commentary or write it if that is part of the plan. The amount of time required and the exact fee should be determined in advance.

Magazines and manufacturers should be contacted at least a year in advance of the show. Sometimes, if their schedule permits, they will provide a commentator as little as three weeks in advance. But this is a matter of luck. To guarantee their services, it is safer to book between August and December of the year before the show when their budget and schedule are being prepared. Inquire into the requirements for a commentator. Most require advertising and merchandise commitments in lieu of fees and it may be necessary to clear the decision with several other people at the store or firm. You should tell them whether or not you have a commentary prepared and give an estimate of how much time for preparation is required. They will probably want to go over the script, but may or may not feel they need to attend a run-through. Also, you will need to know

HOW TO PRODUCE A FASHION SHOW

whether or not to book travel and room accommodations for them. You might want to plan a dinner or small party for the commentator after the show, or give them a token gift. The same arrangements hold for celebrities and personalities. Book well in advance, and determine how much preparation will be needed.

This approach applies to out-of-store or non-retail shows as well. For co-op, trade, specialty, television shows and spectaculars, determine the commitments and fees and book well in advance; find out who should make travel and hotel arrangements and decide on entertainment and gifts.

The Commentary

The purpose of the commentary is to merchandise the clothes—by description, by placing them within the context of fashion and the audience's lifestyle. Each item is presented in its best possible light, not only in terms of what it is, but also in terms of what it does.

The quickest way to lose an audience, however, is to deliver a purely descriptive commentary. The show clothes have already been carefully selected on the basis of impact, which means that they should speak for themselves from the runway. Since a basic description merely tells the audience what it can already see, the commentary should offer new information. The rule of thumb is to go from the general to the particular. A good commentary starts by establishing the fashion feeling of the season. It should specify the current looks in terms of silhouette, proportion, mood, color, fabric, accessories and any distinctive detailing. The commentary should define the clothes in terms of their distinguishing characteristics and differences from last season's. Designers responsible for certain looks can be cited as well. And the whole look can be put into the context of fashion trends over the past few and next few years. Most customers are looking for clothes as investments. Talking about the staying power of certain styles reassures them that they will get mileage out of their purchases. How much detail one goes into and how complicated the generic picture is will be determined by the audience. The more sophisticated it is, the more technical one can be, and the less subsequent commentary is needed.

After the generic introduction, comments about specific outfits can be related to the opening remarks as examples of each trend or look. This technique of going from the general to the particular can be varied by splitting the general comments and using them as introductions to the various categories, rather than at the opening of the commentary. One can also intersperse them at intervals throughout the show.

Over and above the fashion philosophy, the entire commentary will be geared to the audience. The audience determines the approach and the amount of commenting as well as the pace.

A sophisticated audience will understand and want to know the technicalities of fashion. For this kind of audience, the commentary reenforces their own knowledge more than anything else. A minimum of comment is necessary to

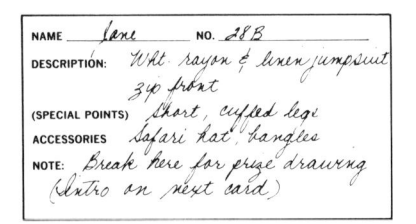

The commentary card should cue the commentator of key points to be mentioned.

COMMENTATOR AND COMMENTARY

make points, and the pace is fast. For a less informed audience, more detail and description can be included. The "how to" show is at the opposite end of the spectrum; the fashion background can be touched on briefly. The commentary will concentrate on analyzing how each look is put together; how it can solve figure problems; when it can be worn, etc. Everything is spelled out and the pace is slower. One of the most demanding audiences is teenagers. The pace must be fast, with a commentary that doesn't make the commentator sound patronizing, or like a teenager herself. The emphasis should be on the inventive ideas and accessories that will individualize the look rather than expensive items.

A stock of ad libs and fillers can be kept separate from the commentary and interjected as needed. An almost endless variety can be written with the most important ones first. If credits are to be given throughout the show, rather than at the break or near the end, they can be used as fillers. These would include store services, facilities and the free-lance experts the store or group has employed or who have donated their services. These would include specifically, hair stylists, makeup artists, accessories personnel; available services such as the restaurant, beauty salon, bridal registry, portrait studio. A charity can take this opportunity to discuss its history, its founders, its benefactors. Fashion points or anecdotes can be used. Departments where various looks for the whole audience can be found—mothers, teens, older women—can be mentioned if it's a seasonal show. At a trade show the designer's outlook, philosophy, recent awards can be used as fillers.

A word should be said about "the pause that refreshes." One way that nerves manifest themselves is an almost uncontrollable desire to talk non-stop. A pause every so often is a refreshing break. A short break allows time for the audience to absorb visual details and digest them; it shouldn't, however, stretch into a hole.

The simplest and most common commentary is put on 5″ × 8″ index cards. The information can cover every point or a series of cues so the commentator covers the highlights. The sequence number and model's name are included along with selling points (they can begin to be filled in during the fitting and later completed). These cards can be held by the commentator, or given to her by the approaching model. The second method guarantees the right card for the right outfit. However, the system is awkward. It puts emphasis on the card system—a mechanical device in the audience's mind, which is unnecessary. Also the model has to walk to the commentator to give her card who may or may not be near the runway. It also leaves the commentator stranded during a hold-up.

Some commentaries are completely ad-libbed by the commentator. This makes for an excellent show, since an audience responds well to a conversational tone and feels that the comments are specifically for them. But it has two potential disadvantages. The commentator, no matter how familiar the clothes are, is likely to omit something important without at least a cue to prompt her memory. Also,

Cards for credits (top) and ad lib or fillers (below) should be kept separate from the commentary cards. The information is worked in as needed.

Types of Commentaries

HOW TO PRODUCE A FASHION SHOW

Having models hand the commentator her card ensures that cards and clothes always match.

very few people can talk for half an hour to forty-five minutes on the same general subject without repeating themselves.

Scripts are used for more elaborate shows. The commentator reads them verbatim. All the elements of the show are cued into them. The models are signalled by certain words, as are the musicians, lighting and sound technicians. In terms of content, the script can be both as generic and specific as the card system. However, it works better when the read comments are used to set the mood, with little effort made to describe. This kind of coordination is vital for an elaborate show. Using a script can be very dramatic, at the same time it lacks spontaneity, which is why the mood-setting function is stressed. Its one great disadvantage shows up if a model enters out of order. Not only is the commentator forced to rustle through pages, but it also throws the music and lighting off. The script, in fact, becomes the controlling factor rather than the commentator in this kind of a show.

Co-commentating is a technique that can be extremely effective. The combination of voices keeps the audience interested. Since male commentators are expected to be less knowledgeable about the intricacies of fashion, a man as co-commentator can act as counterpoint to a woman's descriptive information,

COMMENTATOR AND COMMENTARY

giving the male point-of-view or mentioning some other pertinent aspect.

There is a lot of flexibility with a joint commentary. Each commentator can describe alternate outfits or they can jointly describe each one in various ways. As well as the male comments mentioned, commentators can split the descriptions or can alternate commenting on generic or specific points relating to the outfits. Another variation is to have one commentator introduce the various categories, or open the show with the fashion philosophy and close it with appropriate remarks. However the duties are divided, both commentators should make a real contribution to the show.

Rather than having a second commentator, one can use an emcee to introduce the commentator. The emcee could be a personality or celebrity; or a member of the store's management who welcomes the audience (and commentator, if he's a visiting expert) on behalf of the store. The emcee has the option of returning later for the break, to give away prizes, mention credits and close the show. Or the appearance can be confined to the introduction.

Keeping in mind that the commentary is used to sell, there are a few basic areas to be covered. If cards are used, the category number and model's name should be listed at the top. As you gain experience you'll develop your own system of what to include. A few descriptive points can be listed referring to color and silhouette (if this is put at the top of the list it serves as an immediate verification of the proper model and garment). Selling points that are not visible should be emphasized, such as wash-and-wear or noncrushable fabric. A note relating the garment to general fashion trends can be included, and a comment on the accessories if these are important. Obviously, the points to be included will vary according to the audience. You could mention the outfit in terms of its couture appeal or that it is a budget priced version of a couture item; how it fits into a current wardrobe. Another point to mention is where the garment can be worn or how it can be accessorized to give it a different look.

Price is rarely mentioned in the commentary. If it is expensive and the other clothes seem extremely reasonable, the price could be quoted. Or if it's very inexpensive, an exceptional value. For the most part, price should be ignored to encourage the customer to come to the department and try on the garments.

Any notations about breaks, closes or credits should be made on the card. This way, you can flag the various portions of the show and lead into them, knowing in advance what's coming. (See illustration page 78.)

A script, on the other hand, is a more formal version of a commentary. If it can be given to a copywriter to work up, so much the better. The script should include two columns: the left-hand column shows the scene and model (plus any cues) indications, while the right-hand column shows the commentary with pauses and breaks. The same format is used for co-commentating.

How to Write a Commentary

HOW TO PRODUCE A FASHION SHOW

Shows Without Commentaries

Many of the trade shows have no commentary to speak of; the garments are identified by style numbers. An occasional comment about fabric or availability can be made by a principal of the firm such as designer, publicity director or member of the showroom staff.

In the late Fifties, Mary Quant staged an entire press show without commentary. This developed into a trend in the Sixties, starting with the big press shows in major apparel markets and eventually filtering into local level presentations in smaller cities around the country. The technique is an effective one for communicating excitement, movement and drama—by bypassing words and relying on strong visual and emotional response for impact. Staged properly, these shows can be devastatingly effective. Without careful planning, perfect timing and real expertise, they can be unqualified disasters.

The technique is not suited to every show. The clothes should be young and swinging, and the same can be said for the audience. Styles that are slinky, bias cut—that have motion and vitality—lend themselves to this kind of show. Sound and light experts should be brought in and their respective areas should be closely coordinated with model's movements and a commentator if one is used. Even without a commentary, a commentator may be used in the capacity of an emcee, who introduces the show and possibly certain sections. The key to success here is the coordination—it should be split second perfect.

```
THE FASHION GROUP              COMMENTARY:
AMERICAN READY-TO-WEAR SHOW
NOV. 17, 1972                  GILLIS MAC GIL


    I NEVER DID LEARN ANYTHING ABOUT
ATOMS, BUT IN THE LAST 25 YEARS I'VE
LEARNED A LOT ABOUT MODELING.

    I WAS THERE WHEN THESE FILMS WERE MADE.
WHEN THE GLAMOROUS IMAGE OF THE FASHION
MODEL WAS FIRST COMMUNICATED TO MASS
AMERICA... SOME PEOPLE LEARNED ABOUT
FASHION FROM FOX MOVIETONE NEWS.
```

Large type makes script easier to read. If models, sound and lighting are coordinated with script, commentary can be set up as right-hand column, cues and activities at left.

Setting Up for the Show: The Floor Plan | 9

What the master plan is to the overall show coordination, the floor plan is to the physical setting up for the show. As a visual chart of all the components, it's a good planning aid. As you become more adept at show coordination, the floor plan can be omitted (the jobs connected with setting up can be included in the general master plan).

Following is a list of the various components and their relationship to each other.

The stage is not vital to the show. Many shows are set up without one. Either there is not enough space (if the show is held on a selling floor or in a particular department), the mood is informal, or the impact will come from lighting effects or from the clothes themselves.

The type of show audience and site determines whether or not to have a stage, and what type. Since one function of the stage is to create impact, the larger the show and audience (and therefore the site) the more elaborate the stage must be to create a sense of drama about the clothes. Any show catering to more than fifty people should have a stage. In fact the site should be chosen partly on the basis of whether or not it has, or could accommodate, a stage. With less than fifty in the audience, the models will be easily spotted by everyone, and a stage could diminish the intimacy and personal quality of a small show. On the other hand with over fifty in the audience, the entryway—even a small one—should be defined so that it can be easily seen. This is especially important if you expect the room to be crowded, with the seating close to the entryway.

A formal stage in a theater or an auditorium is ideal. The proscenium or apron can be used for the modeling. However, a stage can be formed by putting tiers or platforms together. These should be very sturdy and covered with heavy fabric or carpeting. A comfortable height is thirty-six inches from the floor—regulation height for most theaters. The tiers or platforms can be lower, of course, as long

The Stage

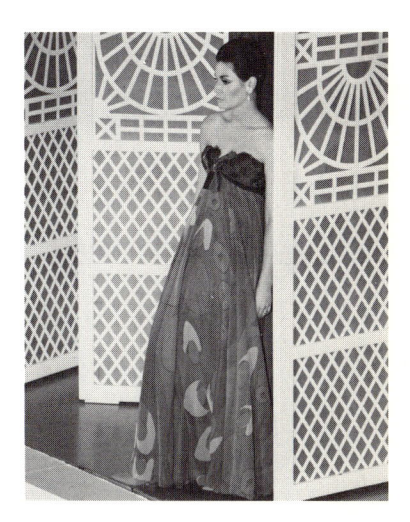

Moveable screens function here as both backdrop and entrances. (Courtesy of The Fashion Group.)

HOW TO PRODUCE A FASHION SHOW

as the models are visible from all points in the audience. An entryway or staging area can be created without these tiers simply by framing a door or entrance.

The Runway

The runway refers to the path the models take from the stage or entryway to the exit. Again, the type and site of the fashion show determine whether or not the runway will simply be a cleared or roped-off area or a raised platform. An elevated runway, offers better visibility to more of the audience whether it is used as a level extension of the stage into the audience, or simply as a series of slightly elevated platforms placed end to end.

Runways come in all different shapes and sizes and can be laid out very imaginatively. The limitations are the available space, the length of time it takes to traverse them, the number of models to be used in the show, and the distance between the exit and the dressing rooms.

There are several basic types, and an infinite number of variations for each runway:

THE T-SHAPED RUNWAY—gets its name from the "T" formed by the stage and runway at right angles to each other. While it is the most common shape, it is also the simplest; models can enter from stage left or right, proceed down the runway and exit from the foot or return to the entry point. It can accommodate a single model or a string of several models. Unless the runway is built wide, it is difficult for two models to appear abreast or pass each other. A simple variation on this shape is to put a platform or widened area at the foot to allow several models to appear there simultaneously or to give them space to make wide turns (a good idea when wide full-length skirts are being shown).

THE Y-SHAPED RUNWAY—two runway arms are placed at angles to the stage, either abutting it or branching out from a connecting runway, to form a "Y" shape. It has the advantage over the T-shaped runway with a very large audience. The model can traverse the entire "Y," which gives a fairly close view of the show pieces to all parts of the audience. Since it is longer, it will usually require more than a minute to walk. Therefore when the "Y" is used, groups of models should appear in close order—otherwise a thirty-piece show could take an hour. Models can also appear together from opposite entrances, walking both arms of the "Y" simultaneously.

"T" AND "Y" VARIATIONS—varying these basic patterns is an easy way to add an element of interest to a show. The long arm of the T-shaped runway can be zigzagged for a new twist. Or the "T" can be up-ended, with models walking straight down the long arm to the perpendicular crosspiece at the end—the platform or stage area being on the audience side rather than the stage side. An "X" or cross can be formed by adding angled center sections.

Another type of runway uses the *theater in the round* principle to involve the

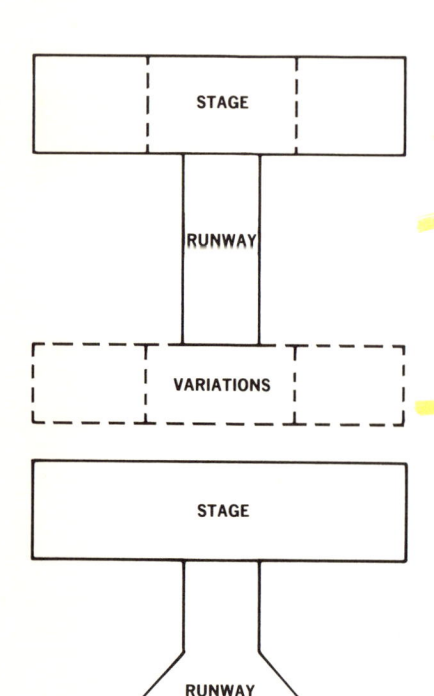

Two of the most basic runway shapes; variations are numerous.

SETTING UP FOR THE SHOW: THE FLOOR PLAN

audience in the show. A platform is set up in the center of the audience where clothes can be seen from all sides simultaneously. A variation of this employs a series of smaller platforms—two, three or four of them—in several different areas of a large room. The platforms can be raised to different heights. This can be complicated in terms of timing, but very dramatic, especially when it is enhanced by spotlighting.

When choosing the type of runway, the flow of traffic (the route the models will take) should be considered. Time and visibility are also key considerations. In terms of visibility, it is important that the model be seen from every seat in the audience. Timewise, the clothes must be exposed long enough to register with the audience, but not long enough to bore them. Each item shown should, like good French cuisine, leave them delighted—and wanting just a little more.

The commentary and route can be coordinated in several ways. The commentator can begin talking either before or after the model appears; she can finish before or after the model exits. She can complete a sentence or an idea after the model exits, or make a generic remark, but *no new information* should be introduced once the model has left the stage. It is frustrating for an audience to try to recall details of what they have seen.

Keeping these options in mind, the model's route should allow sufficient time for the garment to be seen and commentated without dragging the pace. If, for instance, it takes two or three minutes to walk the route, even with the commentator continuing, all pivots can be eliminated or the route shortened to quicken the pace.

THE SELLING FLOOR—The size of departments and aisles vary greatly, even within the same store. Usually, a large department can accommodate a platform and a roped-off area for the runway. If dressing rooms are centrally located, the openings can be used as an entrance onto the runway, doing away with the stage or platform completely. If the seats need to be set up close to the entrance, then the raised platform is necessary to define and emphasize the entrance.

RESTAURANTS—Depending on the layout of the room, the stage can be set up near a wall, with the runway extending into the audience. Some tables can be left in place if refreshments are served or rows of seats can be arranged on either side of the runway. If the area is small, a large stage can be used without a runway—providing the view of the show pieces is unobstructed.

THEATERS AND AUDITORIUMS—Obviously, the runway is restricted if the seats are bolted to the floor. Even so, the center aisle should accommodate a straight runway. If chairs are the folding kind, any of the basic runway formations can be used.

MUSEUMS, MALLS AND OTHER LARGE OPEN AREAS—The only restrictions are keeping the dressing rooms near the entrance and allowing for

The basic "T" becomes an "I." (Love is . . . a wedding with Higbee's and The Bride's *Magazine.)*

Adapting the Stage and Runway

HOW TO PRODUCE A FASHION SHOW

Platforms are laid end-to-end to form a raised runway through selling floor at Lord & Taylor, New York.

electrical outlets. A large stairway is an ideal and dramatic location if it meets the requirements. If the show is being held outdoors, the stage and runway should be sheltered against the wind, and there should be enough speakers to carry the sound to all points of the audience.

Entrances and Exits

The position of entrances and exits is critical to a smooth-flowing show. The nearer they are to the dressing room, the easier it will be to get models out on time, and off the runway in time to change outfits.

Traditionally entrances have been located stage right, stage left and center stage. The right and left entrances offer the greatest flexibility since models can enter and exit from either or both sides, as well as exiting from the foot of the runway. A center entrance is rarely used on a stage. When models make their entrance through a doorway (from the dressing room) or through a frame, it is usually centered against the platform or stage area.

When a full-fledged stage is used, a backdrop with some type of doors or openings can be built to give access onto the stage. This is a more elaborate arrangement, allowing one or several models to make an appearance at the same time, but highly effective. Whatever method is used to hinge or swing these doors, it should guarantee fast, effortless access to the stage.

SETTING UP FOR THE SHOW: THE FLOOR PLAN

Another type of entrance and exit can be created via the use of lighting. Using blackouts and spotlights can create the effect of models appearing and disappearing instantly. However, to avoid having a dazzled model trip or fall, steps and drops should be made as safe as possible.

As mentioned previously, the model room should be as close to the stage as possible. (The diagram on page 89 illustrates the layout of a typical floor plan.) The model's areas should be separate from the pressing area as well as from the area for makeup and hair experts (if they are used). If models are responsible for their own hair and makeup, a lighted mirror, counter top and plenty of electrical outlets should be available to each one. A lot of confusion can be avoided if each model's changes are lined up on a rack in her own dressing area, with accessories located nearby, in the order they'll be worn. If there isn't space, racks can be wheeled into a central area. A theater dressing room is ideal. However, a workable dressing room can be created with a little ingenuity, even in an empty corner with a few screens strategically placed. The best place for individual model's changing and makeup areas is along the walls. Here, they can make all their preparations and still be out of the main flow of traffic. Normally dressing rooms are equipped with long built-in tables under large well-lighted mirrors. The same conditions can be created using desks or tables with mirrors. Electrical outlets should be nearby for heated rollers and curling irons. If each model's clothes are lined up in the same area, her shoes and other accessories can be stored underneath accessible tables. If clothes and accessories are elsewhere, the space can be used to keep her own personal equipment such as foundations and accessories. Each model sheet should be posted in the area—on the side of the mirror, taped to the tabletop or in some other highly visible area.

If makeup and hair stylists are being used, they should be located in a separate area, again with tables and mirrors. This way models can return to their own changing area after makeup and hair are completed with a minimum of congestion.

All pressing should be completed before the models arrive. If there is enough space, the equipment can be pushed into a corner with perhaps a single ironing board open for last minute touch ups. If the dressing room area is small, all pressing equipment should be removed before the models arrive. Any bags, boxes and trunks that the clothes were packed in can be kept in the same area as the other equipment, or stored.

An accessories table can be centrally located and should hold all the extra jewelry, foundations and shoes. In addition, a box full of basic items such as stockings, wigs, rollers, makeup, that have accumulated from past shows should be kept handy. The same area can be used for an emergency kit. The kit should contain an assortment of materials for small repairs and other minor problems. Some of the items would include: needles and thread, scissors, cellophane and

The Model Room

Circular platforms form a stage "in the round." (Courtesy of Hutzler's, Maryland and Glamour *Magazine.)*

HOW TO PRODUCE A FASHION SHOW

masking tape, straight pins, safety pins, paper clips, stapler, pens and pencils, tissues, brushes, rubber bands, hair pins, Band-Aids.

Behind-the-Scenes Personnel

There are a number of unsung heroes involved in the production of a fashion show. They are invisible to the audience but vital to the smooth-running performance.

PRESSERS—They are responsible for pressing and steaming clothes. The major work should be completed after the clothes have been altered and, if it is a short trip, before they are transported to the dressing room. If garments are likely to be crushed in transit, the pressing should be done in the dressing room. If clothes need touching up after the rehearsal or before the show, this too can be done in the dressing room. Members of the alterations department can do the pressing, or anyone handy with an iron (unless it requires a skilled hand for pleats or delicate fabrics).

DRESSERS—Each model should be assigned her own dresser or if necessary, two models can share one. The dresser is responsible for helping the model to change; handling clothes so that they stay as fresh as possible; zipping, buttoning, hiding tags and anything else to expedite the change. She is also responsible for checking the model sheet to ensure the model wears the proper outfit. In addition, she is responsible for caring for the clothes; making sure they're ready to slip on, returning them to the racks in good condition.

Starter (left) watches commentator for cue to send out model. Dresser (right) assists model with a fast change.

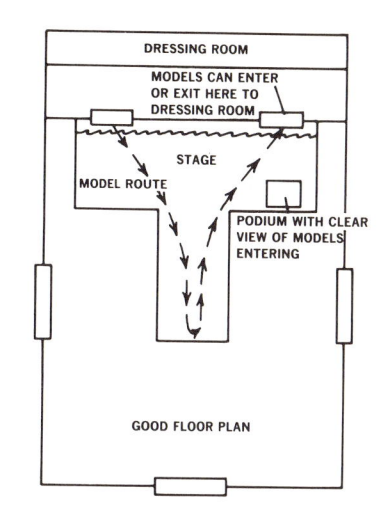

SETTING UP FOR THE SHOW: THE FLOOR PLAN

STARTERS—She's the kingpin of the backstage staff. It is her responsibility to get the models out precisely on schedule, and in order. She works with the final garment sheets or script, following all the written cues, and she—as well as the models—follows the commentator's cues to speed up or slow down the parade. If there is a mishap, the starter signals the commentator to stretch her remarks. While she's lining up the models and sending them out, she's keeping track of how the changes are progressing, so that if there is a hold-up or a particularly fast change she can avert trouble by sending another dresser over. The starter is also responsible for making a final appraisal of the model, checking to make sure tags are out of sight, hair is smooth, etc. If the dressing room and the entry to the runway are far apart, two starters can be used—one to send the models out of the dressing room, the other to send them onto the runway.

STYLISTS—Makeup and hair stylists are used for larger shows. It usually involves a "head man" and one or two assistants plus paraphernalia. They should be accessible, but away from the stream of traffic. Usually each model is styled once at the beginning and then just touched up during the show. Sometimes two or three hair styles will be used on a model if the clothes call for it.

Staging

The staging of the show refers to the mounting or presentation of it, the use of backdrop and props as well as other materials to create a proper background that carries out the mood for the clothes. The purpose of the backdrop or scenery is to enhance the clothes. How elaborate depends entirely on the type of show and the extent of the budget. Only a small amount of staging is needed to provide a background for the clothes; the backdrop and props should not be any more elaborate than necessary to get across the clothes. The staging should be subservient to the clothes, never overshadowing them.

The Backdrop

The simplest backdrop is a frame for the entryway. This is the safest idea if facilities for producing backdrops are limited. The frame can be a trellis, column or large potted plants, which defines the entryway. Backdrops run the gamut in terms of complexity. A painted scene, sometimes with doors for models to walk through, can be used. Fully furnished rooms can be designed, or special effects created by a set designer. Slides and filmstrips can be projected on the back stage wall. A single backdrop for the entire scene or a different one for each scene can be used. In some cases, a revolving stage can set the scene for each category shown.

Props

The props models carry should be minimal. A golf club or tennis tote for an active sportswear show; a balloon or toy for a children's show; a small satchel for travel; an attaché case for career clothes. Anything more elaborate is clumsy for the models to carry and merely competes with the clothes.

HOW TO PRODUCE A FASHION SHOW

Elaborate lighting and staging create drama and excitement in a hotel ballroom for a Z.C.M.I., Salt Lake City, department store show tie-in with The Bride's *Magazine.*

Musicians Musicians can be made more a part of the ambience of the show by positioning them close to the entryway. They should be unobtrusive however, and out of the direct line of vision. A large orchestra can be partially hidden in the pit in front of the stage or screened from view on the far side of the commentator.

Lighting Such a variety of lighting techniques is used that it is difficult to define a single, appropriate area for it. Care should be taken, especially with small spots near the runway, to hood them or place them in such a way that all light is directed toward the runway and not the audience.

Displays Displays connected with the show should be located near a high traffic area—perhaps near doors or stairways or near the refreshment area, if there will be one.

Refreshments If a refreshment table is set up it should be located in another room or as far away from the stage as possible. This avoids noise and traffic problems.

The Floor Plan If you were to draw a blueprint of the show it might look like the diagram on page 89. The placement of the stage and runway in relation to the audience is a determining factor. As mentioned earlier, the podium should be positioned to the left or right of a platform, doorway or frame. The commentator behind it should have a clear view of the entryway, while being able to direct her remarks to the audience. And the public address system at the podium should be connected to amplifiers and electrical outlets without miles of wires and cords exposed.

Store Sponsored Promotion | 10

Promotion and publicity are an inherent part of the fashion show. Often fashion show coordinators can call on advertising, promotion and publicity experts to work on this aspect of the show. Whether or not the coordinator is directly involved in these efforts, she should be aware of all that can be done to insure a successful show.

Promotion and publicity are used to generate awareness and interest in the show (and the organization behind it) and build the type and size of audience that would be most responsive. There are a number of ways to do this, either through the organization or in cooperation with a firm outside it. The facilities within the sponsoring firm, particularly a retailer, should be explored first before an outside firm is approached.

Show invitations are an excellent means of limiting the audience to the type and size that is best while at the same time reaching the greatest number of potential attendees. Unlike print or broadcast advertising, invitations can be sent to a specific, well-defined group of people. And the number of invitations sent can be limited to prevent an overflowing house. In fact, most shows do use either invitations or tickets to control the audience. There is tremendous risk in omitting them, since there is no way of knowing in advance whether fifty or five hundred people will attend. Even if the show is a regular event, there are so many variables that can affect the number of people who attend, that it is pure—and needless—guesswork to estimate it in advance without any means of measuring and controlling it. If individual invitations are omitted, then tickets should definitely be substituted as a control measure.

All invitations should include the show title (which should indicate what type of show it will be), date, time, location, sponsoring group. If RSVP's are required, this should be noted, and any information regarding when and where tickets can be picked up, and the price, if any. If refreshments, prizes or entertainment is

Show Invitations

Invitations—simple or elaborate—should carry through show theme via typeface and layout.

being provided, this can be included as well, although it isn't necessary. The information should be listed as simply and succinctly as possible.

Types of Invitations

There are several types of invitations to choose from, although the rule is in general, the simpler the better. All invitations should be visually appealing and carry through the theme of the show as well as conveying all pertinent information. The theme can be carried out graphically through typeface, color, artwork or in a (very) limited way, through the wording of the copy.

The most commonly used invitation is a block-form formal invitation, either printed or engraved. This can be done in black and white, with or without artwork. It can be made more informal by reworking it slightly, with the same information listed, and by changing the typeface. Either of these styles of invitations can be printed as heavy cards, foldovers, postcards, self-mailers or as statement stuffers.

Beyond these standard forms, the choice of invitation is limited only by time, money and imagination. Heavy card stock, deckle-edged colored papers, matte, glossy, even metallic, finishes, can be used to create the desired effect. Typeface styles can run the gamut from Block to Gothic to Art Deco. Invitations can become as elaborate as Victorian Valentines—and just as expensive to produce. In cases of a limited audience, telegrams or mailgrams can be used, or they can be entirely handwritten.

Whether it's a consumer or trade show invitations, programs and press kits are a key part of the promotion. Here, Seibel & Stern carry through a Broadway show feeling with "Playfrills" theme.

STORE SPONSORED PROMOTION

> # bloomingdale's
> ## white plains
> ### INVITES YOU TO ATTEND THE OPENING SERIES OF SPECIAL EVENTS FOR FALL 1975
>
> All Events Will Be Held In The
> Provence Restaurant Unless Otherwise Indicated
> Doors Open At 9:00 A.M. For
> Coffee & Pastry
> Lectures Begin At 9:30 A.M.
>
> **Thursday, Oct. 16** — **RUDOLPH NABEL** Of Nabel's Nurseries, Inc. will share some of his expert knowledge on the care and feeding of indoor houseplants with special notes on the needs and wants of the *plants* and the varied home environments in which they must live.
>
> **Tuesday, Oct. 21** — **PABLO'S PALETTE** — The award-winning Pablo Manzoni, creative director of Elizabeth Arden, best known as a make-up artist, will talk about Fall and Winter beauty trends, as well as demonstrating basic make-up techniques. Pablo will be available to answer questions in the Cosmetic Department immediately following his lecture.
>
> **Wednesday, Oct. 22** — **MAKE IT FIT** — Ruth Amiel and Happy Gerhard, authors of "Finally it Fits"(Quadrangle), take the mystery out of patternmaking and illustrate how to make clothes that fit your specific figure needs by making simple pattern adjustments.

Seasonal calendars show dates to make advance planning easier for customers.

When invitations are being used also as tickets they can be numbered; perforated portions can carry matching numbers. Lines that are included for names and addresses serve several purposes: as admission tickets, door prize drawing stubs and as permanent attendance records to be used for future mailings.

Invitations should be mailed ten days to two weeks prior to the show. This allows people time to make plans, yet it is close enough to the show date to remain fresh in their minds. In the case of charity events, three to four weeks should be allowed. The extra time is needed to actively sell the tickets, or chances, since they are usually expensive and require telephone and personal calls.

The easiest—and obvious—method of distribution is by mail. Store mailing lists of charge account and other customers are highly prized and closely guarded. The least expensive means of distribution is to send invitations with monthly statements. The disadvantages are that the timing may not be ideal. They may reach people too early or too late. There is also the risk that the invitations will be overlooked among the other mailing pieces with the statement. Invitations as statement stuffers are best used in conjunction with a separate mailing. Either as an advance notice or as a follow-up reminder to the invitation mailing. In addition, many stores periodically send calendars of events to customers. These should always include a listing of shows. Some stores have sophisticated lists that

Distribution of Invitations

HOW TO PRODUCE A FASHION SHOW

> Missoni for Spring '73
> February 22nd at Bloomingdale's
> Ondine Restaurant
> 1111 Franklin Avenue, Garden City
> 9:30 a.m. — Admission card

Tickets are a necessity if the size of the audience has to be controlled.

are coded by zip code, age, family size, even income bracket. If a seasonal or other broad-interest show is being mounted, a general mailing is fine. If a very specific target audience is desirable, a customer list broken out by code can be used.

When a large crowd is desirable, other lists can be used to supplement the customer list. Most stores develop names from each show or promotion that is run by distributing cards that ask if the individual would like to be notified of future events (with space provided for the name of a friend). These same cards can be left out in the various departments, on main floor counter tops and other high traffic areas. Over a period of time, this is an excellent way to build a high-response mailing list.

Another source of names is a local or national list house, where names can be bought by the thousand—with coded lists available by zip code or other characteristics. If this is one of several sources of names being used, however, there could be a high percentage of duplication.

List houses are a source for charities or other non-retail organizations. If a store will part with its list, it is the best source of all. Other lists might be obtained from local merchants and specialty stores, country clubs and political or social organizations. In addition, invitations can be sent to these same groups in bulk for distribution. They are especially apt to do this if they are participating in a tie-in promotion or donating prizes for the show.

In highly specialized departments, such as bridal, couture or furs, the sales personnel may keep their own lists of customers. They often, particularly in the bridal area, keep newspaper clippings, such as wedding and birth announcements, women's page features, new arrivals in a small community of potential customers.

When mailing invitations without tickets, the type or caliber of the mailing list will determine the response. With mailings against a "qualified" list, that is people who have some interest in the show such as store customers or people who have attended earlier shows, you can count on a fifty percent response, so you can send double the quantity you hope to have attend. When an unqualified list is used, such as any mailing list bought from a list house, you can count on a small percentage to respond. Unless it has been used before, the names are unknown and it is far more difficult to determine the response percentage.

Large mailings can go out using printed address labels, if necessary, although typed envelopes are preferable, if slightly more expensive and time-consuming. Charity events or small specialty shows should have hand-addressed envelopes since a personalized quality is important. For the same reason, hand-stamped rather than machine-cancelled envelopes should be used.

Tickets

Tickets are another method of controlling the response and can also be used for door prize drawing stubs or reserved seating arrangements. If the show is being promoted through general advertising rather than individual invitations, a control becomes doubly important. If tickets are free, attendance can range from fifty

STORE SPONSORED PROMOTION

to eighty percent of the total number of tickets distributed; depending on who picks them up and how difficult it is to get them. Generally, the more specialized the show, the higher the response will be against distributed tickets. And if tickets are available upon request from a specific department in the store, this will further increase the percentage of response. Whereas, tickets readily available in highly convenient places will have a lower percentage.

If there is an admission charge, the number of tickets given out will be lower, but the percentage who attend will be higher. In this case, you can allow between ten to fifteen percent no-shows, and overprint to that extent.

Large rolls of standard tickets can be purchased from stationery stores, printers, and other sources. If a theater or civic center is used, they may have their own numbered tickets which correspond to seat numbers. Specially printed tickets can include numbers for prize drawings and space for names and addresses for future mailings.

Store Giveaways

There are a number of small favors, tokens and gifts that can be given away in order to build interest in the show and reward the audience.

Any organization can order small items and imprint them with the name of the firm or the event. Pencils, pens (which are helpful for checking off on the program outfits to be tried on), shopping bags, calendars, address books and a wide variety of items like this can be used as token gifts. They can be designed to carry out the show theme. These can be purchased from premium houses, if local stationers do not carry them.

A retailer can order favors to be given away in quantity from vendors who supply the store on a regular basis. Buyers are usually familiar with the type of merchandise that is suitable and who will supply it. Fragrance and cosmetic firms offer sample sizes; small leather goods, scarfs and other accessories make good gift items, too.

Retailers also have a large selection of goods and services to choose from within the store. With the exception of trips or cars, the giveaways should be stocked, since this is an excellent opportunity to promote the store. Large items can come directly from stock—wardrobes worth up to several hundred dollars or individual items of apparel can be given away as well as housewares, sporting goods, china, glass, flatware, table accessories and gift certificates. Store services such as haircuts, facials, make overs, portraits make very desirable gifts.

Non-retail groups are more limited. They need to solicit free gifts or have to buy them from the stores or manufacturers lending their clothes. All gifts should be non-competitive, to avoid a head-on comparison among manufacturers. Never two irons or jackets, but an iron and a blender, a jacket and a dress.

Programs

Programs are used as a guide to the garments or groups being shown. While the programs are helpful to the audience and can enhance the mood and theme of

HOW TO PRODUCE A FASHION SHOW

the show, they aren't necessary. In fact, many smaller shows eliminate them completely.

The amount of information covered in the program and the way it is presented varies greatly. Although programs can use copy to set the mood or give background information, the shortest, most straightforward description is the best—certainly the easiest for the audience to follow. The best examples list garments in order of appearance with a one- or two-line description—a clear identification without going into detail; the model's name needn't be listed unless amateurs are being used as a drawing card for benefits, children's shows, etc. Since more people are likely to be tempted to go into the departments and try on the garments without knowing their price, including it is optional; the majority don't. If one of the main points of the show is budget or practicality, however, then prices can be listed. (If prices are not given in the program, they should certainly not be mentioned by the commentator.)

Other optional information to be given is credit to the designer. Some stores prefer to promote their fashions under their own labels, others buy name designers because of their following. If a designer (or manufacturer) has an established clientele or if it is a designer show, then definitely include the name.

Accessories need not be listed at all. Occasionally an important handbag, belt or scarf makes the outfit, in which case a quick reference to it can be made.

Programs can be as simple as a single mimeographed sheet or as complex as an elaborate memento of the show. As with invitations, the artwork, typeface and color scheme of the program should relate to the theme of the show. A standard presentation is to show the title of the show, name of sponsor and date on the front, with credits and services on the back. This can be printed on heavy card stock with the description of the show pieces inside, either printed directly on the card stock or printed or mimeographed on separate sheets and inserted into the program folder. If the garment sequence is not definite it is quicker and safer to print the description sheets separately and insert them between the outer covers at the last minute.

Programs for benefits are usually elaborate brochures with heavily embossed or printed covers. Here space can be set aside to describe the goals and benefits of the organization, its officers' or directors' functions and lavish credit given to all donors. Extra revenue can be generated by selling the program (to defer extra costs for paper, printing, etc.) or advertising space to various donors and patrons —individuals, local and national business firms. Once the units for space and their rates are set, letters and calls can be made to potential advertisers soliciting their support. A letter can be drafted mentioning the advantages of advertising, the readers who will see it and the fact that it's tax deductible. If the benefit is an annual event, programs can be overprinted each year so that samples of past programs are available to help sell the current ones. Local merchants are the obvious source of ads, but national organizations—especially those with local-

Bloomingdale's, Short Hills, promotes Redbook *Magazine tie-in to shoppers via children's in-store display.*

STORE SPONSORED PROMOTION

In-store display promoting Mademoiselle *Magazine tie-in.*

level affiliations—should be contacted as well. Usually a letter or kit full of information and a follow-up call will be sufficient.

Timing the printing of the programs will depend on the printer. Unless it's a very elaborate job, a week to ten days will be enough time. And often printers can produce it in a matter of hours, although you pay a premium for this service.

Store Displays

The majority of the audience for a retail show will be drawn from the store's regular clientele. The best place to start promoting the show is within the store itself.

WINDOWS—Several prominent windows can be devoted to the show exclusively. Clothes displayed can be duplicates of show garments or reasonable facsimiles. (The window can also include a card with information on the show and some of the prizes to be given away.) The backdrop can carry out the theme by using ideas that will be incorporated into the backdrop of the show. Other windows can simply display placards with pertinent details of time, place, etc. Independent organizations can solicit window displays from participating retailers which contain some or all of the elements listed above.

IN-STORE DISPLAYS—Displays promoting the show can be spotted throughout the store. Island displays can be simplified versions of window displays. Placards, counter cards and floor stands can be set up giving show details. They can be layed out like the invitations and if there is publicity value with a photo of the commentator or emcee. These are simple to produce in quantity and should be displayed in several areas of the main floor, in main aisles and elevators, near escalators, in fitting and ladies rooms. In-store displays should be concentrated in areas from which show merchandise has been taken, and from related areas. A children's wear show should be promoted in the women's departments, sportswear shows in sporting goods and active sportswear, a bridal show in housewares, china, luggage, jewelry. This, in addition to their respective departments.

Timing Displays

Both window and in-store displays should go up about a week prior to the show. This gives the customer a chance to plan her schedule. Any earlier than a week and she's likely to forget. Furthermore, floor space is valuable to a retailer and a week for display space is long enough for a single promotional event.

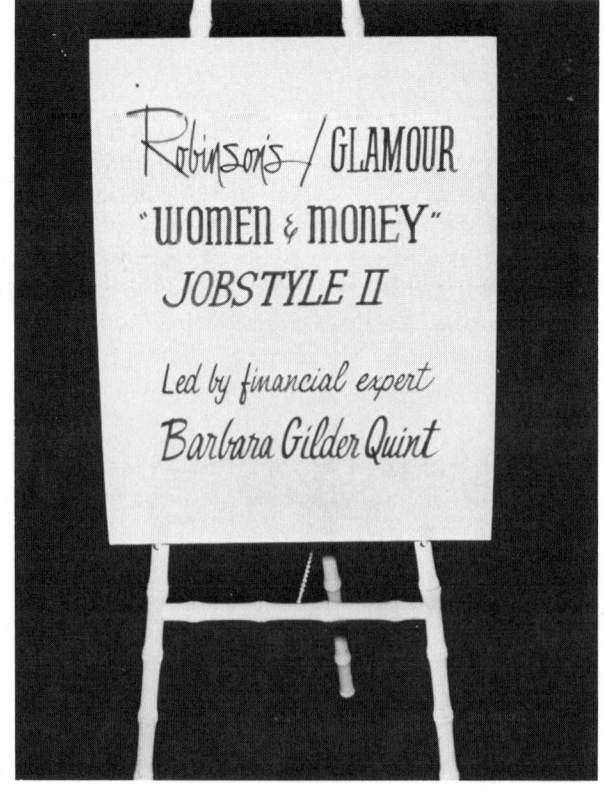

Window display and floor placard promote upcoming shows. Left: Mademoiselle *Magazine tie-in with Gimbels. Right:* Glamour *Magazine tie-in with J.W. Robinson's, Southern California.*

Promotional Tie-Ins and Giveaways | 11

A tie-in is a cooperative effort between two or more firms for their mutual benefit. It usually involves a trade-off of merchandise or services in return for advertising, publicity, or goodwill. If a store or an organization approaches another firm for a tie-in for the show, it must be able to demonstrate that it can offer something substantial in return, preferably something that will result in sales.

There are several types of tie-ins that can be taken advantage of: large and small door prizes and giveaways, personnel and services. All of these should benefit the show in terms of traffic, excitement and prestige. If publicity is to benefit the retailer to the fullest extent, the giveaways will be items carried in the store.

As with small items to be purchased, most buyers know vendors who have the particular merchandise that is suitable for door prizes, and which ones can be approached. Again the best sources are cosmetics and fragrance manufacturers for sample-sized colognes, perfumes, purse sprays, trial-sized cosmetics and treatment products. A designer might contribute one or more of his designs. Fiber companies can often contribute goods or specially purchased products.

Silver, china, glassware manufacturers are also good sources; as are small appliance and housewares manufacturers. Local restaurants and theaters and other entertainment spots might be persuaded to contribute. Several of the airlines have a policy of contributing part or all of a vacation package. And, laws permitting, wines or liquors make good giveaways.

On large prize items—heavy appliances, cars, travel, furs, expensive apparel, the manufacturer may require partial payment, either to defray factory costs or for preparation and shipment. It is wise to get an exact estimate in advance on what the charges will be and to alert prize winners as to their tax liability and to whether or not they have the option of converting these prizes into cash or a cash equivalent. Housewares and appliance manufacturers and their industry organizations can also be called on for brochures, pamphlets, demonstrators as well as merchandise.

Prizes

Magazines offer a wealth of materials to be given away at tie-in promotions. (Courtesy of Glamour *Magazine.)*

HOW TO PRODUCE A FASHION SHOW

Left: Paris designers work with Air France to entertain American buyers with an in-flight "trade" show. (Courtesy of Air France.) Right: A tie-in with a magazine can increase the audience size two or three times over. Here, Seventeen Magazine/Frederick & Nelson, Seattle, promotion.

These manufacturers should not be constantly approached as their promotional budgets are limited. But many manufacturers, particularly local merchants, welcome the publicity, so it should not be too difficult to get their cooperation. Maximum exposure should be given to the gift items. Store purchased or sponsored items can be listed by category (i.e., blender, toaster-oven, suede jacket). For obvious reasons, all donated items should be credited by the manufacturer's name and/or trademark. This builds excitement and encourages more manufacturers to participate in the future. Wherever possible, show ads should list contributing manufacturers. They should also be listed on the back of the programs. The prizes (or duplicates) or a list of donors can be included in window and in-store displays and a display table can be set up near the entrance to the show area. Donors should be credited during the show and they can be touted during the drawing when the prizes are given away. Photos of all the prizes can be sent to the donors to document the publicity and exposure and they can be used to approach donors for future shows.

Stores are in the best position to request gifts from the suppliers, since they buy regularly from them. Also they have the facilities to widely advertise the show —more than an independent organization producing the show. A well-known

100

PROMOTIONAL TIE-INS AND GIVEAWAYS

charity has a good chance of receiving donations as well (the chances of success are much greater if an executive of the donating firm is personally approached). Many firms, particularly the larger ones, are sensitive to public relations and therefore are very receptive to lending a hand when it will result in goodwill. Trade shows, on the other hand, will fare poorly when it comes to donations, since the audience comes from within the industry—there is neither wide exposure nor community spirit to recommend the donation. Far and away, the best bet for a trade show coordinator in search of promotional aids are the fabric and fiber companies that supply the manufacturer—or the fiber company if the show is produced by a fabric supplier.

Many of the fashion and service publications tie in regularly with retailers around the country. They rarely work with non-retailers unless it is a large charity or indirectly involves a prestigious store. Their merchandise or promotion department has a staff of experienced commentators who can also supply ideas for themes, summaries of current fashion trends, quotable copy blurbs, ad mats and layouts and previews of future issues of publication. There are major advantages to using a magazine commentator (see *Types and Sources of Commentators*, Chapter 8) and participating in a tie-in, in terms of prestige value and audience appeal. A few publications will also provide videotaped or filmed fashion presentations. There are a variety of other items available as well, such as quantities of current issues, program covers, shopping bags or totes, brochures and quantities of prizes from various manufacturers who advertise in the publication.

Media Tie-Ins

Magazines sometimes supply giveaways from their major advertisers to stores. (Courtesy of Mademoiselle *Magazine).*

101

HOW TO PRODUCE A FASHION SHOW

Dunlap's gives both their Youth Board and local models a prominent position in their ad for a Co-Op Show with Seventeen Magazine.

DUNLAP'S and SEVENTEEN MAGAZINE

present the SCHOOLBOUND FASHION REVUE
Tuesday, Aug. 5, at 2 p.m. in the Municipal Auditorium

You'll find everything new in fall fashion, music old and new by The Electric Ear, with dancing and fashions as seen in *Seventeen* presented by models and Dunlap's '74-'75 Youth Board — all in one exciting, entertaining show! Fill out an application to be on the '75-'76 Youth Board and register for Dunlap's gift certificates. Admission to all the fun is free ... see YOU there!

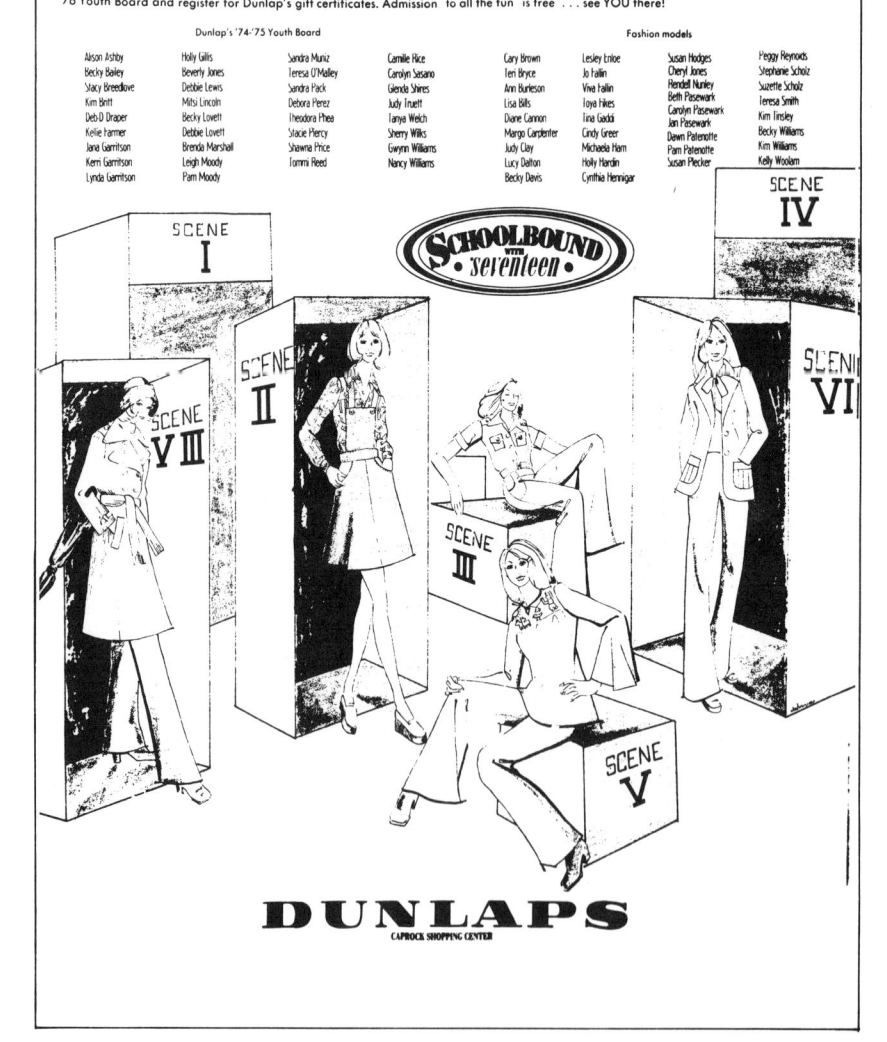

Dunlap's '74-'75 Youth Board

Alison Ashby	Holly Gillis	Sandra Muniz	Camille Rice	Gary Brown	Lesley Enloe	Susan Hodges
Becky Bailey	Beverly Jones	Teresa O'Malley	Carolyn Sassano	Teri Bryce	Jo Fallin	Cheryl Jones
Stacy Breedlove	Debbie Lewis	Sandra Pack	Glenda Shires	Ann Burleson	Vive Fallin	Hendell Nunley
Kim Britt	Mitsi Lincoln	Debora Perez	Judy Truett	Lisa Bills	Toya Hikes	Beth Pasewark
Deb D Draper	Becky Lovett	Theodora Phea	Tanya Welch	Diane Cannon	Tina Gadai	Carolyn Pasewark
Kellie Farmer	Debbie Lovett	Stacie Piercy	Sherry Wilks	Margo Carpenter	Cindy Greer	Jan Pasewark
Jana Garritson	Brenda Marshall	Shawna Price	Gwynn Williams	Judy Clay	Michaela Ham	Dawn Patenotte
Kerri Garritson	Leigh Moody	Tommi Reed	Nancy Williams	Lucy Dalton	Holly Hardin	Pam Patenotte
Lynda Garritson	Pam Moody			Becky Davis	Cynthia Hennigar	Susan Plecker

Fashion models: Peggy Reynolds, Stephanie Scholz, Suzette Scholz, Teresa Smith, Kim Tinsley, Becky Williams, Kim Williams, Kelly Woolam

SCENE I · SCENE II · SCENE III · SCENE IV · SCENE V · SCENE VII · SCENE VIII

Schoolbound with *seventeen*

DUNLAPS
CAPROCK SHOPPING CENTER

102

PROMOTIONAL TIE-INS AND GIVEAWAYS

Seventeen Magazine show at Rich's, Atlanta, features clothes from editorial pages. Other tie-ins might use store-selected merchandise.

A few stores feel that it is a disadvantage to work with a publication. Retailers have sunk thousands of dollars into building a unique fashion image through careful advertising and buying and do not feel they need to lean on a fashion publication to give them added authority in this area. Most retailers, however, not only believe they benefit from this kind of tie-in, but rely on publications to draw the big audiences that make a major show profitable.

Magazines usually require a store to commit to advertising space or buy merchandise being shown in the advertising or editorial pages of upcoming issues. (It is a big plus for the show to have a group of featured merchandise—the commentator can give it a big play and emphasize that it is being featured nationally—it is even better if the magazine issues being distributed carry the clothes.) Their requirements may also cover a certain amount of local advertising back-up featuring their logo or cover shot as well. All requirements, particularly when they affect the advertising budget or buyer's commitments, should be settled in advance. The magazine should be contacted six to twelve months in advance to guarantee their participation on a preferred date.

Occasionally a magazine will sponsor a traveling trunk show. The clothes they send around the country—sometimes accompanied by a commentator, sometimes with models—are looks from upcoming editorial pages. There is often a very strong and distinctive fashion philosophy behind it and the issue in which the clothes appear is heavily promoted. The advantages of this kind of show are that the store need not buy all the merchandise, it benefits from the fashion reputation of the publication and its promotion, and much of the organizational

HOW TO PRODUCE A FASHION SHOW

work behind the show is done by the magazine. The drawbacks are that unless the featured merchandise is in stock, sales may be lost, even if the looks are presented as generic. Also, the clothes represent the fashion thinking and expertise of the magazine and carries its personal stamp rather than the store's.

Many magazines publish a schedule or list of the shows and stores they are tying in with—whether or not they send a commentator. Be sure to ask to be included on this list if it's their practice.

Manufacturer Tie-Ins

Apparel manufacturers, fiber and fabric companies have promotional aids available to retailers in the form of personnel, goods and money. Anyone involved with show promotion should make a thorough study of vendors who supply the store and of the textile companies who will work directly with a retailer. Some of the designers or other staff members are available as commentators for shows, or will make guest appearances as part of a retail promotion. Most manufacturers, however, only do this for favored accounts, and it means that a store must build their show around the designs of one manufacturer. For a small show, featuring a single couture or middle market line, this may be desirable. For a larger show, especially a seasonal show, a single designer is not strong enough and it is not to a store's advantage to be associated with one manufacturer exclusively (in the audience's mind). If a well-known designer is putting in an appearance to show his line, a small tea or cocktail party can be planned for him as part of the overall promotion, in addition to other private entertainment. This can be used to introduce some of his staunchest patrons to him.

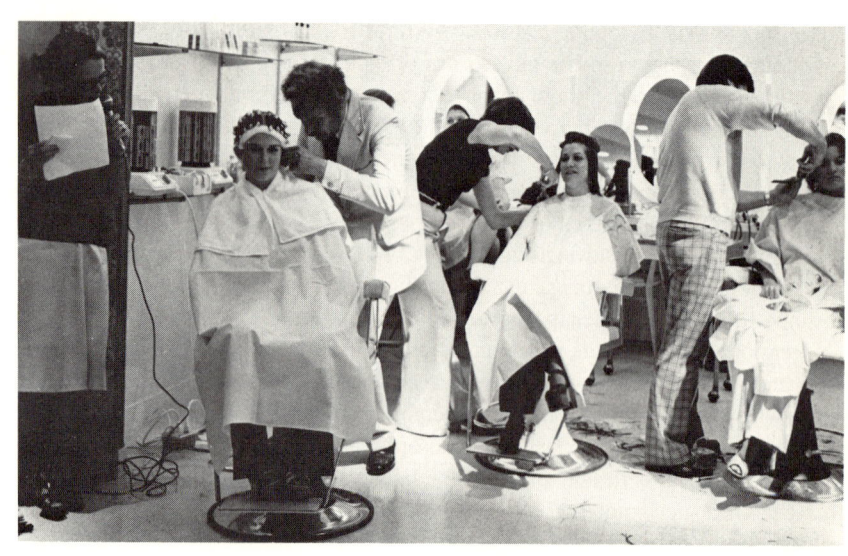

Above: Mademoiselle *Magazine workshop highlights use of accessories. Right:* Seventeen *Magazine tie-in promotes consultations and hair styling at Frederick & Nelson, Seattle.*

104

PROMOTIONAL TIE-INS AND GIVEAWAYS

To capitalize on tie-in, credit magazines and prize donors in newspaper ads promoting show. (Courtesy of Saks Fifth Avenue and Redbook *Magazine.)*

Textile firms are good sources of background information. They will occasionally participate in a retail tie-in although they prefer to work with manufacturers —their customers The design, promotion and merchandising staffs of these companies have an excellent broadscale grasp of what is happening in fashion and can make a real contribution to the show. The only disadvantage is that the audience is more familiar with the names of apparel manufacturers. And, as with

105

HOW TO PRODUCE A FASHION SHOW

This page, department display reproduces Redbook *Magazine pages as part of children's show promotion. Next page, the* Redbook *spread that inspired the show theme. (Copyright,* Redbook *Magazine.)*

106

PROMOTIONAL TIE-INS AND GIVEAWAYS

apparel manufacturers, their personnel are likely to concentrate on promoting their own fabrics and trademarks.

An ideal event for textile participation would be a home sewing show. The over-the-counter fabric companies can supply a commentator and clothes, and experts can teach basic and advance sewing techniques as part of a major promotion. Some of them also have commentators who can put on excellent hatbox shows, again using their own fabrics.

Both manufacturers and textile companies offer other promotional support—chiefly in the form of advertising dollars. While budgets have shrunk in recent years, many firms still offer money for cooperative advertising. Textile industry associations also offer these services. To qualify for these dollars, a store may be required to buy a quota or feature the company's logo or merchandise heavily. The store will have to decide how much of their advertising or buying money they are willing to commit in order to qualify.

These firms offer many of the same things as the magazines: press kits, summaries of fashion philosophy, ad mats, suggested layouts and copy, photos, ideas for themes.

HOW TO PRODUCE A FASHION SHOW

Local Media　　Local television and radio are excellent sources of free coverage for the show. As with local businessmen, they are most likely to offer it if they are involved in the show.

Both television and radio stations can contribute personalities who can commentate, co-commentate or act as emcees. Some of the most successful teen shows have employed local deejays to put the clothes across. These personalities are happy to plug their appearances on a show. A woman's program personality also makes a good commentator. The stations can announce where to pick up tickets. Either the station or the agent of a personality should be contacted regarding availability, fees, etc.

Newspapers are less likely to tie in officially with a show. Rarely are their reporters available for personal appearances of this type. And while they are always eager for advertising, they are extremely reluctant to bargain away their editorial space. They may offer their name for a charity event but this is the extent of their support (see *Working with the Press*, Chapter 12).

Local Experts　　There are a number of individuals and firms that are necessary, or add something, to a show. Quite often they are willing to donate their services or charge a token fee in return for the exposure the show offers.

Makeup artists, whether employed by a national cosmetics firm or operating independently, can be called upon to donate their services. Also, hair stylists. Local jewelers and furriers can also be persuaded to lend items from stock, although if the retailer sponsoring the show has departments competitive with these outside firms, it is preferable to take the merchandise from their own stock. Florists are willing to contribute bouquets or arrangements. Caterers and musicians are less likely to donate their time, but it is worth approaching them.

If a major promotion is planned around the show, other business firms can be approached. Banks, real estate brokers, travel agents, insurance firms are just a few of the firms that can provide valuable information to customers.

Advertising and Publicity | 12

Both advertising and publicity are critical to the success of the show. No matter how alluring or entertaining the clothes and presentation, if no one knows about the show, no one attends. The purpose of advertising and publicity, as with promotions and tie-ins, is to generate interest and build an audience. Advertising, on the one hand, is usually paid for by the organization that sponsors the show, and therefore there is control over the information given out and the timing. Publicity, because it is free and at the discretion of someone else, requires careful planning and presentation to guarantee maximum positive exposure at the best time to benefit the show.

Advertising is one of the best methods of generating interest in the show. It can be used to reinforce individual invitations. When invitations are omitted, advertising becomes the primary means of promoting the show.

Regardless of the space or length of the ad, or the vehicle carrying it, every ad should contain the following:

ESSENTIAL INFORMATION—name of sponsor, title (must indicate content), time and location. This is the minimum required information. Other elements are optional, but strengthen the appeal. If budget and space permit, additional information can be included. Promotional copy on show attractions: clothes, prizes, giveaways, etc.

OPTIONAL INFORMATION—artwork (photo, illustration, graphic designs carrying out the show theme), personalities, prizes and giveaways, merchandise descriptions (brief), refreshments.

Ads can run anywhere from ten days before—to the day of the show. Within this time frame, store policy, personal experience or research on customer awareness and response, budget and availability of space will determine the frequency

Advertising

Print ads promoting show can be all-type or illustrated depending on their size.

Timing

HOW TO PRODUCE A FASHION SHOW

Creative, inexpensive "display" advertising. The Boston Store, Fayetteville, uses back of bus to promote "Fashion Show on Wheels" in cooperation with Seventeen Magazine.

of the ads. Both print (newspapers, local magazines, house organs or other publications) and broadcast (television and radio) ads depend on a certain sense of immediacy to sell their content, so the best (biggest and strongest) ads should appear the day before the show. The Sunday prior to the show is also good, since papers enjoy their largest readership then. Early ads can be small teasers with the barest details about the show. These will serve to pre-sell the show, with larger ads later used to motivate the reader or listener to act (make a decision to attend; reserve or buy tickets). The element of immediacy is even more important in broadcast than in print; awareness and response on television and radio spots will be considerably higher the few days prior to the show.

Size and Frequency

The basic principles regarding size and frequency apply to both broadcast and print media, although they are handled differently for newspapers than for television and radio.

The budget and the number of people to be reached are important factors. Obviously, the bigger the fashion show, the larger the size and greater the frequency of ads. However, even without a large budget, there are ways of squeezing maximum impact out of the advertising.

ADVERTISING AND PUBLICITY

Print advertising space can vary from full pages (spreads—two facing pages—are available, but rarely used) down to a few lines. Broadcast advertising generally varies from a minute to fifteen seconds. The budget can be stretched by running large and small ads. Since greater awareness is achieved by running many small ads rather than a few large ones, the emphasis can be placed on teaser ads repeated at frequent intervals. For instance, a show budget might cover the cost of three full page newspaper ads. One of those pages might equal ten teaser ads. So the campaign for the show might be kicked off with a full page ad in the Sunday paper, followed by teaser ads scattered throughout the paper during the week, with the second full page ad appearing the day before or the day of the show.

Another way to stretch the budget, or when a budget doesn't exist, is to add teasers carrying essential information to other regularly scheduled ads (in the case of retailers). An ear (corner) of a larger newspaper ad can be devoted to show information. A single column extension can also be used. With broadcast, a super slide (copy line) can be used at the tail end of a spot, or a voiceover giving details of the show.

In terms of frequency, ad costs determine the total space or time bought, but the greatest number of ads, regardless of size, should be bunched near the date of the show.

Retailers have a wide selection of media to use since they are dealing with the consumer. Charities have the same options on media vehicles. Although they are in a better position than retailers to receive free space, they cannot tag onto regularly scheduled ads.

Advertising for trade shows is more limited as to the choice of vehicles. Trade journals or papers are the best place to run ads, since these publications reach the target audience. These ads can be simpler than consumer ads; all-type ads are the rule, rather than the exception.

Newspaper Advertising

Most retailers have favored newspaper advertising over television and radio because it is less expensive while reaching a large audience. With a large budget, both large and small space ads can be prepared. A combination of full, half and quarter page size ads can be interspersed with one and two column ads and ears which can be tacked onto regularly scheduled apparel ads. As mentioned before, where the budget is smaller, ads can be kept small and run frequently. This saves on production costs as well as space. The larger ads can be laid out using artwork, whereas, the smaller ads are best confined to all type.

Since many people read only certain parts of a newspaper, the positioning of the ads is important. Most people reading the women's page will have an interest in a fashion show (as opposed to those reading the financial or real estate sections, where the interest would be marginal at best) therefore a good spot for a women's show ad is on or opposite this page. The sports or financial sections would be

HOW TO PRODUCE A FASHION SHOW

excellent positions for a men's wear show. A teen show ad could appear near a regular column on new records. The entertainment or television listings get high readership and would be suited to a broad-interest show. Some newspapers may have page-by-page readership data that can be used to determine the positioning of ads.

Newspaper ads can also appear up front (far forward) in the publication—in the news section. Pages 2, 3, and 4 are good spots because most people picking up the paper will at least glance at these pages.

If co-op or tie-in ads are being run, at least one of the larger ads must include this information, not only to benefit from the tie-in, but as part of the arrangement with the participating firm. With a co-op, a certain percentage of the ad space, usually specified in advance, must be devoted to the participant. On a tie-in, the ad can feature the names of participating manufacturers. A listing of products or prizes and brief descriptions can be included, but it is not necessary.

Radio Advertising

As with newspapers, shorter, more frequent ad spots produce better results. Fifteen second spots can be prepared, with the basic show information given briefly. One minute and thirty second spots can also be used, with more complete details. A co-op ad should mention the name of the co-sponsor or participant. Tie-ins are generally confined to newspaper ads, so manufacturers' names need not be included. A reference to door prizes should be made however, since this

Good press releases and good press relations should generate editorial coverage. (Courtesy of Women's Wear Daily*.)*

The Sexy sell

A sexier-than-usual approach to market week shows — even in sleepwear — took place Wednesday in the Rainbow Room, New York, as a collection called LovinWear was presented with breakfast, for about 100 buyers.

What exactly is LovinWear? "Sexy loungewear for men and women who want to be loved," touted the sponsoring Celanese Corp. To illustrate the point, male and female models frolicked in a variety of jumpsuits and body wraps and otherwise paired-up in simulated "real-life" situations.

Reaction to the less-than-pristine (but tongue-in-cheek) concept: "It was well presented and well done," said Mary Ricciardi, robe buyer for John Wanamaker's.

Altman's fashion director Anita Gallo had her eyes on the clothes: "Both the men's and women's clothes were beautiful and just right for the Altman customer. But I just didn't notice the presentation nearly as much as the clothes. When you see so many of these things, it's impossible to judge them any other way."

Anita Gallo and George Hanley; the Big Ogle

Photos by Lynn Karlin

is an attraction. In terms of timing, the newspaper principle of positioning holds true here, too. Ads should be scheduled during programs of interest to a potential audience. Rock shows can be used to attract teen listeners; women's programs for wives and mothers; early morning or news programs for working women or men. Peak listening times are excellent as well.

Television Advertising

More and more retailers are using television on a regular basis—for apparel as well as hard goods. However, because of the expense, few will prepare and run an ad solely to promote a fashion show no matter how large. If television ads have been already prepared or scheduled, it is an easy matter to include a slide or super slide (copy lines) at the end—a line or two of copy giving show details. The same scheduling as for newspaper and radio applies. "Prime time" for the ads is peak watching periods or shows of interest to the desired show audience.

Advertising Budgets

Ad budgets are usually allocated in advance, and never seem to be enough, which is why budget-stretching techniques are necessary. When making them up, be sure to budget for the production of the ads as well as the space. This preparation can sometimes represent a big percentage of the budget. Also, check to see if there is a frequency discount offered by the media for firms that advertise with them regularly.

Publicity

As with advertising and promotion, the purpose of publicity is to build interest in the show and attract an audience. On a long-range basis, good publicity will result in a reputation for interesting, exciting clothes and events which snowballs over a period of time. This is particularly beneficial to a retailer interested in developing a larger and steady year-round clientele.

Publicity includes write-ups, mentions, plugs, feature articles given the show and sponsor by editors. This kind of extra coverage is free and the editor is implicitly endorsing or recommending the show. If a newspaper editor, radio or television personality has a large following, it is a real plus for the show. At the same time, it requires extra effort to get this space, because these editors are only prepared to cover events of interest to their own audience.

Therefore it is critical that an angle or slant on the information is developed that will make it newsworthy. All publicity material released must have:
1. A usable general slant, gimmick or angle that recommends it.
2. A specific slant for individual editors.

The more these two principles are followed, the greater the chance that the material will be picked up and used.

If the theme has tremendous impact, it can be used as the basis of the publicity release. If it is broad or not attention-getting, a new angle should be worked up —the more intriguing or controversial the better. If photos are used, the show merchandise should be combed for the best and newest looks.

HOW TO PRODUCE A FASHION SHOW

Radio spots are an excellent way of reaching teens and young women. (Courtesy of Glamour *Magazine.)*

GLAMOUR

Suggested 30 Sec. Radio Spot*

GO WEST! GO ROCKY MOUNTAIN WEST with (the) _____ mall and GLAMOUR Magazine. Enjoy _____ full days of travel-time "How-To" tips that include fashion shows, beauty clinics, art and photography exhibits, contests, prizes and more! All packed with the frontier flavor of a Rocky Mountain revelation. Relive the past and celebrate the future of this exciting part of America. Join us _____ through _____ at the _____ mall. And don't forget to look to the April issue of GLAMOUR Magazine for the fresh easy look of Rocky Mountain fashion and beauty.

*Suggested background music: John Denver's "Rocky Mountain High". RCA Records.

Sources of Publicity

The woman's page editor of one or several local newspapers or magazines is the ideal source. Also, women's television and radio programs, disc jockeys will pick up releases.

Publicity Materials

The basic publicity tools include: Press Releases, Publicity Photos and Captions, Press Kits.

PRESS RELEASES—These usually follow a standard format. A specific release date indicating when the story can be broken (closer to show time, the line can read "for immediate release"); a contact and phone number for further details can be listed on the top of the release. An attention-getting headline should follow—guaranteeing that the reader will go on to the first sentence. All the essential information on the show (sponsor, title, time and location) should

ADVERTISING AND PUBLICITY

Photos and copy can be assembled in a press kit or distributed individually. (Courtesy of Clovis Ruffin of Ruffinwear.)

```
RUFFINWEAR SUMMER '76        Contact:  Jeanne Chappell
The Kreisler Group                     Advertising & Publicity
550 Seventh Avenue                     Director
New York City   10018                  212-221-0644

    FOR IMMEDIATE RELEASE

Clovis Ruffin loves no-zipper summer clothes and does them better
than anyone!

At left - that rare thing, the perfect dress for a summer event,
like a wedding.  A dressy, lean, t-shirt inspired tent body and
the smallest cap eyelet sleeves is belted at the top of the hip
with a self sash.  Buttons down the back (that shouldn't all be
buttoned) make it easy for you to show off your great American legs
from a whole new perspective.
```

HOW TO PRODUCE A FASHION SHOW

appear in the first sentence. This way, the reader has all the details without having to read further. The following paragraphs should highlight the fashion news and excitement in a little more detail.

The release should be strong and concise. It should never exceed a page—two or three paragraphs, double-spaced are sufficient. It is important to keep in mind that the press release is designed to pique interest—not to summarize the show.

The above approach is used for releases in general. If two or three releases are being produced for individual editors, a little more tailoring is required. Knowing the editor and the style of her column is important. The release can be written in her style with the slant she is likely to use. By emphasizing separate aspects of the shows for different editors, each has an "exclusive" story. If an editor consistently reports on controversial high fashion, this should be emphasized in her release. If her readers expect a practical, down-to-earth approach, this should be the slant. The headline should be as close as possible to her own editorial style.

PUBLICITY PHOTOS AND CAPTIONS—These photos should show no more than three garments in order to reproduce strongly and without confusion. They should have simple (solid-colored, if possible) backgrounds. Newspaper photos should be sharp and clear with a glossy finish. Keep in mind that a lot of detail drops out in the printing process, so strong contrasts and simple lines are best. Photos for television should also be clear, but with a matte or dull finish to avoid glare. Each photo should have a brief description attached, along with a release date and contact. The copy can be attached to the back and folded over the front.

PRESS KITS—These usually consist of a cover sheet set up as a standard press release with several photos and captions of show highlights. They are usually used at trade shows or press showings, when there are too many editors to prepare individual releases. A store can send these to editors after the show to be used as the basis for a follow-up feature.

The opening lines of a press release should grab the attention, contain the essence of the show and invite the reader to read on. (Courtesy of Ohrbach's.)

Working with the Press

Local editors should be alerted several weeks in advance of the show so they can hold space to cover it. Every person who represents a potential source of editorial coverage should be alerted. They should be called and invited to interview and photograph visiting personalities connected with the show. Models and clothes should be made available for photographing.

Either personal invitations or tickets should be given to all of them, and ringside seats reserved. Every effort should be made to make their coverage as easy and as painless as possible.

Visiting commentators or personalities should be briefed on their individual slants, and it never hurts to save a small piece of "inside" information (on the record, of course) to give them regarding the show, or on fashion or consumer trends.

Shows Requiring Special Handling | 13

All fashion shows, whether a back-to-school or a mature woman's show, have certain things in common. The preceding chapters have dealt with basic preparations regarding planning schedules, determining type, site and location of the show, organizing merchandise to be shown, advertising and publicizing the show.

Preparations for most shows, especially the seasonal presentations, will follow these general directions without much variation. Most specialty shows, on the other hand, require some adaptation. In addition, a knowledge of the specific market being covered as well as the targeted audience is important. It's virtually impossible to avoid the pitfalls without it. If the fashion show coordinator doesn't have the firsthand knowledge, an expert or consultant can be brought in. A retail buyer is an excellent source of information for a store show. In fact, it will be primarily retailers who present these specialty shows. (These same retailers can be contacted through independent groups for charity, co-op, television or other types of specialty shows, particularly if they will be participating in the show with merchandise.) The rule about firsthand knowledge holds true for trade shows as well, although presumably anyone attempting a trade show has had at least an apprenticeship in the specific market in which he or she is working.

Shows may be specialized because of the market being covered, such as children's or bridal wear. It may also require different handling because of the audience, such as for a teen show; or it may be specialized by degree of difficulty and organization, as with the spectacular. Following are some of the specialty shows and their particular requirements.

The bridal show is possibly the most demanding in terms of the specialized knowledge and technical details involved. Bridal wear itself is romantic and, especially when presented in whole wedding parties, certainly has dramatic impact. However, despite the fact that bridal wear has become more diverse recently, it is still difficult to avoid being repetitive. This problem is made worse

Long trains and veils on bridal gowns restrict models to all but the simplest movements. (Love is . . . a wedding with Higbee's and The Bride's *Magazine.)*

The Bridal Show

HOW TO PRODUCE A FASHION SHOW

by the fact that details, fabrics and pale colors (wedding gowns, especially) tend to fade out on the runway. Furthermore, since the appeal of the merchandise is essentially to the emotions, it is difficult to offer the hard information necessary in the commentary, and still retain the emotional impact.

Bridal shows require careful selection and presentation of merchandise with just enough commentary to enhance the appeal—neither overly descriptive nor gushy.

EXPERT ADVICE—This is a must, either from the bridal consultant or the buyer. Weddings represent the last bastion of rigid etiquette and only an expert knows the intricacies of train and veil lengths, varying degrees of formality, what the groom and ushers wear and when.

BASIC PLANNING—A bridal show is invariably a parade. The audience will be future brides, their mothers, friends and a scattering of prospective grooms. Smaller shows can be held in-store, but the bridal show is a case where a hotel or restaurant will enhance the appeal and provide a natural setting for the clothes. As to timing, most shows are held in January and February for spring and summer; August and September for fall and winter. This is done to allow for six to eight week deliveries on gowns, plus fittings. Evenings and Saturday afternoons are the best times since many in the audience are working.

As with ready-to-wear, the merchandise selection should be based on a variety of styles and prices. Gowns with strongly defined details such as lace cutouts, pearl and paillette trim, color, reembroidered lace medallions, braid trim are good choices. More subtle details will go unseen. Maids' gowns present less of a problem and several styles can be shown in the entire color range available. Mothers of the bride and groom, fathers, ushers, pages as well as maids and flower girls can make up whole wedding parties. Accessories should be kept to a minimum: a strand of pearls, gloves and shoes. Travel and work clothes, party, at-home wear as well as a few well chosen peignoir and gown sets should also be included in the bridal show. Informal gowns and styles for the "remarried" bride should be included as well since this is a growing category.

RUN-OFF—The sequence should include groups of entire wedding parties, as has been already mentioned, as well as single brides, and bride and maid combinations. Groupings have more importance in a bridal show, since the overall effect is so important. The finale can consist of an especially opulent tableau or a parade of the last gowns shown (save the most spectacular 'till last).

MODELS—Amateurs are preferred in a bridal show for several reasons. First, the clothes restrict movement to all but the simplest movements, which an amateur can handle easily. Second, youth and ingenuousness are more important than professional aplomb, and finally, using real brides-to-be has more audience appeal, and encourages models to buy from the store represented in the show.

SHOWS REQUIRING SPECIAL HANDLING

(Models should be warned against turning or pivoting, and shown how to handle stairs.)

COMMENTARY—Descriptive information should be at a minimum. Even the most varied bridal shows can include a dozen or more "A-line empires in peau de soie with reembroidered lace motifs" all with slight variations. It is more to the point to define the clothes in terms of their proper season and the style of wedding they are suited to. Each of the silhouettes and the various fabrics can be mentioned once or twice to show variety, and the rest of the talk should concentrate on etiquette, tips for organizing the wedding and reception and the different train, sleeve and neckline changes that can be made on each gown. Ad libs can include wedding myths, legends, store services.

COMMENTATOR—Bridal magazine representatives, bridal designers (or ready-to-wear designers who have produced bridal collections), the store bridal consultant or buyer, or the fashion coordinator can be used as well as local personalities. The commentator should have expertise in this area, but a novice can do it if well coached. In this case, descriptive cards made up during fittings are doubly important.

DRESSERS—They should be instructed not to button every button—use zippers only, or pins if necessary. Pressing is time-consuming, so gowns should be handled with extra care.

STAGE AND BACKDROP—Since the clothes themselves are so dramatic, the simpler the backdrop the better. A frame or arch will suffice, or flowers alone. The runway should be simple and short with no sharp turns or step stairs to negotiate. The surface and edges should be smooth so veils, trains and hems won't catch. Small spotlights should be angled across the runway rather than down onto it, in order to highlight detail—but only if it can be done without glaring into the eyes of people in the audience.

INVITATIONS AND ADS—Both can be designed like formal wedding invitations, with all-type and illustrated ads following the ready-to-wear schedule and timing. Special mailings can be made from lists culled from recent newspaper engagement announcements. General mailings are a waste of time and money since the percentage of brides is so small (this by the way holds true for most of the specialty shows). Name and address cards can be kept in the bridal and housewares departments to be filled out, since prospective brides begin shopping six months to a year in advance of the wedding date.

PROMOTIONAL TIE-INS AND GIVEAWAYS—Mementos are great draws at bridal shows, so giveaways are important. And since brides will be furnishing homes and fitting out kitchens, housewares and small appliances make excellent prizes and serve to promote these departments.

HOW TO PRODUCE A FASHION SHOW

The Home Sewing Show

The Home Sewing Show takes a "how to" approach. Above: Simplicity Patterns commentator demonstrates how to use instruction sheets. Right: Women lineup to be measured for muslin patterns.

This area has rapidly closed the fashion gap. Both pattern companies and fabric manufacturers are quick to bring out new looks. The merchandise selection can be exciting and varied. And a number of simplified and advanced techniques have been introduced to enable the home sewer to achieve a professional look.

Home sewing shows can be fashion parades or "hatbox" shows, but most are staged as "how to" presentations. Since many sewers are learning to sew for others —their children or grandchildren—or have decided to sew for themselves, the "how to" emphasis is usually on how to fit. It can also illustrate how to augment a ready-to-wear wardrobe (especially when you know the audience will include many occasional sewers), how to change the same basic look with simple pattern alterations or with different fabric or trim.

EXPERT ADVICE—Unless the fashion coordinator is an expert sewer herself and familiar with the latest techniques as well as the new fabrics, she should simply oversee the planning and leave the specific details, and the commentary as well, to the buyer, department head or visiting expert.

BASIC PLANNING—If space permits, the home sewing show should be held in the department itself, since the fabrics on display serve as a great sales stimulus. If a large turnout is expected or if a luncheon is planned, the show can be held in an auditorium or restaurant, or an out-of-store location. To handle large crowds and still keep the show in the department, several presentations a day can be scheduled over a two- or three-day period with tickets sold to control attendance.

Demonstrations on pattern fitting and alteration, basic tailoring and designer

SHOWS REQUIRING SPECIAL HANDLING

techniques are usually set up after the show. These can be handled in the department as well—if you plan to fit a number of people in muslin, individual fittings can be scheduled for customers every fifteen minutes.

RUN-OFF—The run-off can be determined by setting up an Ideal Chart and working with pattern envelopes. Because of the amount of detail covered, each piece takes longer to commentate. The show should contain about thirty pieces with the presentation lasting between thirty and forty-five minutes. Once the clothes have been sewn and fitted, the basic preparation for a ready-to-wear show can be followed. At least one dress rehearsal should be scheduled to carefully check the fit of the garments. This is particularly important if it is a trunk show, where the clothes have been originally fitted on different models.

MODELS—Because of the slower pace three models, if they are professionals, are sufficient to show the clothes. Five or six amateurs can show the same number of pieces.

COMMENTARY—This is much more detailed for a home sewing show than for a ready-to-wear show. It should certainly cover the current fashion trends with

Local deejay attracts crowds of teens with a live broadcast from Frederick & Nelson, Seattle. (Courtesy of Seventeen *Magazine.)*

emphasis on fabric, color, texture, silhouette and trim. In addition, it should include how to handle new fabrics, their drape and techniques or special attachments needed. Pattern envelopes with notes and information on models can be used in lieu of or in addition to commentary cards.

COMMENTATOR—Representatives from pattern and textile companies, magazines, home economics teachers or department personnel make good commentators.

STAGE AND BACKDROP—Since the bolts of fabric and wall displays are sufficient the backdrop can be kept to a minimum.

INVITATIONS AND ADS—Small space ads can be run prior to the show and a mailing can be made up from a special list of regular home sewing customers developed through having patrons fill out cards. General lists or charge account lists can be used as well, but be aware that there is the risk of luring ready-to-wear customers away from this more lucrative area.

PROMOTIONAL TIE-INS AND GIVEAWAYS—Both pattern companies and textile manufacturers offer traveling shows and commentators which makes sense if a store or school doesn't have the facilities for putting together shows on a large scale or a regular basis. These same companies, as well as notions and sewing machine manufacturers, should be approached for giveaways and door prizes.

As part of the promotional effort, local home economics teachers can be contacted since they are in a position to recommend the shop or department to students. Previews can be set up with demonstrations covering the handling of new fabrics, or they can be given prominent seats at the regular show.

The Teen Show

The teen show can be staged as a fashion parade, spectacular or "how to" show. It is one of the most challenging shows to produce since it must grab and hold the interest of a young and vital audience. Because it requires a creative approach, it can also be one of the most interesting and rewarding to present.

BASIC PLANNING—February and March are good periods for a spring and summer show; August and September for fall and winter. New merchandise is in the store and teens are thinking about their wardrobes for the coming season. An auditorium or large open in-store area is suitable as well as a club, restaurant or local place patronized by teens. Music is important; if it's a big show, space should be allowed for discotheque equipment or a band. Some sort of refreshments can be served. An evening is best, although early afternoon if school is out is good, too.

A fast pace should be maintained throughout the show with groupings used to give variety. Boring this audience is easy—and the kiss of death as far as future

SHOWS REQUIRING SPECIAL HANDLING

sales are concerned. Merchandise can be concentrated around school, holiday and party clothes with sportswear and beach wear getting more emphasis for spring and summer.

MODELS—Nonprofessional teen models are preferable to pros—as a draw for the audience. Teens tend to be slow changers, so changes should be kept to two or three at the most with plenty of time between changes. This means arranging for many more models than usual. Also with the additional number of people in the dressing room and the nervousness and excitement likely to be generated, extra supervision should be arranged. Working with teen models can be made easier by scheduling extra rehearsals and being very explicit about directions. A written set of instructions can be issued outlining model's responsibilities, attitude, behavior as well as directions for the runway and dates and times for models to appear. Males should be included as models. It is an opportunity to promote another department and heightens the audience appeal.

COMMENTARY—It should be informative rather than descriptive and as fast paced and straightforward as possible without being "cute," "hip" or patronizing in any way.

COMMENTATOR—A local deejay or television teen show personality is ideal. Teen magazine commentators have appeal as well as a store or local person that the audience can identify with.

STAGE AND BACKDROP—The whole presentation should be exciting and dynamic. If a backdrop is used, it should have a contemporary theme. Lighting and music should be as sophisticated as possible. The lighting can be coordinated with a good tape system, if the music isn't live. Any of the runway configurations can be used provided they aren't so long or elaborate that they slow the pace.

INVITATIONS AND ADS—Again, good mailing lists can be compiled from cards filled out in the departments, or from school lists. Following the ready-to-wear scheduling, large and small space newspaper ads can be run and both invitations and ads should carry through the theme in a bold and exciting way.

PROMOTIONAL TIE-INS AND GIVEAWAYS—Favors of fragrance or cosmetics are always welcome. An appealing door prize might be a wardrobe or item of clothing, a record album, show tickets.

The College Show

These are usually held in August and early September before students go away. A co-op show staged at a college could be produced later, after school opens and in early spring. The most common presentation is a parade, with tight pacing. A broad variety of merchandise can be included, to cover clothing needed at schools in various parts of the country. Again, models can be amateurs because of their appeal, but professional models, who are credible as college girls, can be

HOW TO PRODUCE A FASHION SHOW

Clowns, balloons, candy contribute to a relaxed spontaneity at a Children's Show.

used. Many stores have college boards from which models as well as advice regarding college etiquette and social practices can be drawn from.

The School Show

The markets covered would include teen, high school or college clothes. What distinguishes this type of show is the location—within the school or university. If the site and the potential audience is large enough, sponsorship can be co-oped among several groups. One has the advantage of working with the institution's facilities—gym, auditorium, theater—and its staff. The campus newspaper, bulletin boards, television and radio stations can be used to generate interest.

The Children's Show

It is simply impossible to exercise the same control over a children's show that you can over other types. A children's show, young children being what they are (as models or as part of the audience), has to be more informal than other shows. The planning should be flexible to accommodate surprises—pleasant or otherwise. The special arrangements for this type of show include providing supervision for models and entertainment for the audience. Much of the entertainment will come from the antics of the models. As to supervision—it is critical. Without it, those endearing little mishaps can rapidly turn into major disasters.

Most stores will use amateur models since this guarantees a big turnout of families and friends. However, professional child models know what is expected

SHOWS REQUIRING SPECIAL HANDLING

of them and are more reliable. Each model should have his own dresser who will also supervise him. Mothers who are a calming or controlling influence can be used in the dressing room. Great tact has to be exercised to keep mothers, who seem to disrupt plans or routines, in the audience.

A starter is especially important in a children's show to maintain the pace. If the dressing room is any distance from the stage, then a second starter should be posted at the entry to the runway in case coaxing is needed. In addition to these starters, someone should be posted at the foot of the runway in case of trouble there, out of reach of other show personnel.

The backdrop can reproduce a children's theme, such as a party or the circus. This is one show where entertainment is an enormous asset. It is a lure for children and helps keep them occupied and happy. It can be done very simply with a clown, magician or puppets. Costumes can be rented and worn by staff members (no experience is necessary—but they should be at ease with children). The theme of the show and the entertainment can be coordinated, with lollipops and balloons as giveaways. Drawings can be held for toys, games, clothing or gift certificates.

The sequence should be kept as smooth as possible. Two children at a time can show, not only because it is more interesting, but the two tend to reassure each other.

The commentary should emphasize practicality, especially ease of care, and versatility.

The general list of charge account customers can be used for an invitation mailing, since most families will have some interest in a children's show.

Commentary for a Mature Woman's Show should emphasize basic points such as color and proportion.

The Mature Woman's Show

These shows are best done as "how to" or parade shows at the beginning of a season. The site should be small and intimate to preserve a friendly atmosphere.

The whole thrust should be to update or acquaint women who may lack confidence in their own tastes or feel out of touch with current trends. Merchandise should not be too high fashion or extreme and each look should be broken down to show components and how the total look is achieved. A "how to" show can concentrate on figure camouflage, versatility, new proportions, accessorizing, along with tips on beauty and foundations. Groupings can demonstrate "how to" points or show do's and don'ts.

Models should be mature, attractive, but always women whom the audience can identify with.

Commentary should be informative, although some descriptive information can be added, particularly on color, texture and synthetic fibers older women may not be familiar with. The commentator should be someone whose viewpoint and authority they will accept.

Once again the department card system is a good way to develop a mailing list. If charge account customers can be identified by age, this is a good source.

HOW TO PRODUCE A FASHION SHOW

For impact, ads for Co-Op Shows should list co-sponsors and participants as well as scheduled events. Here, Maas Bros. advertises their bridal promotion in conjunction with Modern Bride.

Cosmetic or fragrance items make good favors and clothing or gift certificates (or a make over session) make good prizes.

Coffee or tea, or a luncheon increases the informal, friendly atmosphere and gives women in the audience a chance to discuss and weigh what they have seen.

The "Hatbox" or "Bandbox" Show

This is probably the easiest show to set up. Arrangements consist of reserving the commentator (and his hatbox of merchandise), promoting the show through advertisements and invitations and preparing a small area within the department for the presentation. Some pressing or accessorizing may be needed, but it will

SHOWS REQUIRING SPECIAL HANDLING

be minimal. A larger area—the auditorium, perhaps—can be used, but the unique feature of this presentation is that it is perfectly suited to a small, contained space.

The Co-Op Show

This type of show can be mounted as a parade or spectacular and can be held in a mall, store or other area. Since several firms co-sponsor this show and merchandise comes from many sources, the special arrangements involved have to do with extra coordination (and communication). Furthermore, these shows tend to be large promotions, often lasting several days, and attracting large crowds. Preparations are done farther in advance and require a greater degree of follow-up on detail.

The *key* to organizing a co-op show is to appoint a single chief coordinator or chairman, whose authority will be supreme. A committee or staff can be set up with each member being responsible for one aspect of the preparation. The amount of merchandise contributed by each show sponsor can be decided by the group.

Other preparations follow the basic plan. If a huge audience is needed to make the show successful, short television spots can be used as well as newspapers and other less expensive promotional vehicles.

The Charity Benefit

Fashion shows as fund raisers, either as spectaculars or as part of larger promotions such as luncheons, dinners, card parties, have proven very successful.

The extra expense and effort of producing a spectacular may be justified in producing a charity benefit, since the audience will be well entertained in return for its contributions. Again, the committee approach is the easiest way to organize the preparations. If the show requires complicated routines, professional models or performers should be used. Otherwise, the show coordinator or committee should line up prominent local women as models to insure an affluent audience.

Arrangements for tickets to be printed and sold are made well in advance. Raffle tickets can be sold as well. And an auction can be held to generate additional revenue. Charity patrons, local firms and individuals can be approached for raffle and auction items. A group or committee can be responsible for selling the program and the advertising space in it.

The Designer Show

Unless the store has bought a major portion of the designer's line, a designer show is usually a trunk show. A trunk show allows the retailer to sell many styles which the designer brings with them, but which the store has not bought. The designer show may be an informal showing or a parade, depending on whether the designer appeals to an elite or a broad group. The purpose of the show is to enhance the prestige of the store and attract specific customers as well as to make sales.

HOW TO PRODUCE A FASHION SHOW

Famous couples, on a screen and on the runway, were used to attract the right audience to Saks Fifth Avenue for a show benefitting the American Cancer Society.

Many designers make trips around the country to "service" their retail clients (this is invariably a retail show). It adds to the show to have the designers commentate and they will probably deliver their own commentary. However, be prepared for the artistic temperament to assert itself. Arrangements may have to be redone—and at the last minute—to suit the designer.

If local models are being used, a fitting should be arranged before the presentation. Also, arrangements to entertain the designer may have to be made. This could take the form of a small luncheon or supper, or a reception with their customers following the show.

The Trunk Show This type of show may be built around a "name" designer (see *The Designer Show*) or any manufacturer or possibly one of the fashion magazines. The advantage to any trunk show is the ability to sell styles not bought by the store, thereby stretching the buying budget. The preparation is the same as for the designer show, although the entertainment is optional. If a commentator is not provided, a list covering the merchandise to be shown should be obtained in advance so that the commentary can be worked up.

SHOWS REQUIRING SPECIAL HANDLING

The Trade Show

The purpose of a trade show is to present merchandise *within* the industry rather than to the consumer. The audience at an apparel manufacturer's show will be retail buyers. Fabric firms might present to apparel designers; fiber firms may present to mills (to "place their ideas with them") or to retailers (to promote their fibers and the apparel made from their fibers). All the trade shows are covered by fashion editors as well. This audience is professional and therefore demanding. The information transmitted must be factual. At the same time it should reflect the current mood of the consumer—how the customer wants to feel, how she wants to look in the merchandise, etc. Retailers particularly must be given a viewpoint that can be promoted.

Many trade shows use a theme and a presentation that emphasizes the current mood. In fact, this approach will affect every aspect of the presentation. It means that the coordinator must know fashion in general and her market specifically. She has to be able to translate the mood into the theme of the show. She must

Carol Lawrence and Howard Keel (left) and Helen Hayes (right) model in a benefit for the March of Dimes. (Courtesy of The National Foundation of the March of Dimes.)

129

Period costumes are part of an Adolfo showing to benefit The Museum of the City of New York. (Courtesy of Saks Fifth Avenue.)

be able to distinguish between last year's sexy (nailheads) and this year's sexy (flowers) innovations.

BASIC PLANNING—This parallels the steps already outlined with some variations. In planning the merchandise, the Ideal Chart may be broken down into groups within one market. For instance: bathing suits might be the entire merchandise category with sub-categories such as one-piece, two-piece, mix and match tops and bottoms, cover-ups.

RUN-OFF—Rather than deciding the run-off by shifting merchandise on racks, it may be necessary to plan from sketches or polaroids, if garments are not available at the time. Also, there may not be a large enough selection to "pull"

SHOWS REQUIRING SPECIAL HANDLING

A press release for a designer's show (and the commentary) should emphasize his special look and fashion philosophy. (Courtesy of Clovis Ruffin of Ruffinwear.)

CLOVIS RUFFIN

Summer is the most exciting time to be a woman. (Looking wonderful is so simple: it's as easy as slipping out of bed and into something beautiful and bare, adding a touch of makeup and a few accessories). Summer's the time of year no woman can resist buying a dress!

Summer colors are the richest and this year Clovis' colors are even more so (like colors before chemicals were invented): greens that lean towards blue, reds that lean toward rose, sun-bleached beiges, dreamy sky blues, browns that turn a soft henna.

Ignoring last summer's infatuation with big looks, Clovis builds his summer collection on slim, almost A-line bodies (that never have a waist seam) with the belt a size too big, resting on the top of the hip, that elongates the torso and gives a slight blouson effect.

Summer always thrives on a collection of T-shirts and skirts. And for 1976, Clovis has put together a colorful collection of the newest coordinated sportswear - short sleeved tops in signature stripes and solids with flattering batteaux necks and surprising small details (lacings, ribs) that never overpower the slimmest, most wearable summer

HOW TO PRODUCE A FASHION SHOW

Choreographer, producer, director and musical director watch model dancers practice routines for a Deering Milliken Breakfast Show.

double the amount of merchandise to be shown; a few extra garments will be enough protection, as long as duplications are avoided.

The length of time for the actual presentation should be relatively short. As little as fifteen minutes for a between season show to thirty minutes, which is an excellent length for a show. Garments can be shown at the rate of one or two per minute—faster if groupings are used.

MODELS—Professionals are always used in a trade show. They can show three or four pieces each, depending on their expertise and how easily the changes can be made.

COMMENTATOR—Since the commentary reflects the firm's viewpoint, the commentator can be a member of the firm, although a personality or celebrity can be brought in for a more elaborate show.

COMMENTARY—The commentary should give details but the emphasis

SHOWS REQUIRING SPECIAL HANDLING

should be on mood. It should—like a consumer show—leave the audience hungry for a closer look. If the show is elaborate, a written script can be used, but more and more trade shows are commentated using notes and cue cards and rely on an (almost) spontaneous, off-the-cuff delivery to give the presentation more vitality and immediacy.

PUBLICITY—This should include a publicity release at least, preferably a press kit with photos and releases which can be picked up or referred to by the editors.

INVITATIONS—These should be sent out three weeks in advance. The invitation should carry through the show theme—previewing and pre-selling the show. Special invitations and special seats should be given to the press.

GIVEAWAYS—No giveaways are necessary. But a program, in the form of a resource list so that garments to be seen or bought later can be checked off, should be provided.

The Spectacular

This is the most elaborate type of fashion show. Fabulous stages and backdrops, skits, music, dancing, all can be used in a spectacular. All are designed to entertain and amuse as well as to sell.

The spectacular is the most difficult and costly type of show. Often it is coordinated with a charity organization or civic group for purposes of fund raising. Or as a major "event" to create publicity and excitement for a manufacturer or designer or fiber organization. The spectacular although tricky and demanding has its own rewards. Despite the extra work, the store or sponsoring group has the opportunity to present expensive merchandise to fashion-conscious customers and at the same time, if it is for charity, the retailer demonstrates its concern for and involvement in community projects.

The show coordinator must function as a producer/director in her own right, making sure everything goes off on schedule. In addition to the normal mechanical preparations, the spectacular usually requires tight record keeping for tickets and receipts for contribution, raffles (special gifts or door prizes) and giveaways.

Since an important aspect of the show is the dramatization of the clothes, a producer or director is brought in, as well as a choreographer, set designer, musical director, lighting expert, speakers, professional emcee, copywriters and even professional actors.

Working with a producer has the advantage of insuring an exciting, professionally executed show, while removing much of the responsibility for details—and legwork—from the coordinator. Select a producer whose work you know. If you are unfamiliar with someone who is recommended, ask to see examples of his work and check with people he has worked with.

The producer should not be responsible for the concept. This should come from the coordinator who knows the sponsoring firm, the audience, the fashion

Elaborate Deering Milliken program lists garment resources, headshots and background on principle actors and actresses participating in show. (Left and above: Courtesy of Deering Milliken Inc.)

133

HOW TO PRODUCE A FASHION SHOW

FASHION	CENTRAL AREA	BEAUTY	FASHION		CENTRAL AREA
					BEAUTY

Top: A Mademoiselle Magazine workshop includes simultaneous seminars on fashion and beauty. Below: Suggested floor plans for workshops supplied in advance to retailers. (Courtesy of Mademoiselle *Magazine.)*

philosophy, the response she wants to leave the audience with, etc. Furthermore, many producers tend to repeat or vary slightly their past successes. The coordinator can develop a distinctive theme for the show, and should be able to convey it as specifically as possible. The producer will flesh it out and execute it. Many producers work with their own choreographers, designers and lighting technicians, which saves the coordinator time and trouble of hiring them separately. As each phase is worked out, you can approve it. Sketches should be submitted by the designer for the backdrop or stage as well as for a floor plan.

The glittering backdrops, choreography, script, clothing selection—the whole ambience—must be calculated to create the maximum impact.

The merchandise planning, advertising, publicity and invitations follow the steps mentioned in earlier discussions of types of shows. In terms of structure the spectacular may be an elaborate fashion parade; it may involve skits or tableaux, dancing or any other form of presentation a stage can accommodate. In terms of merchandise selection the range could cover couture or designer clothes, dresses (afternoon and evening). A charity event calls for expensive, luxurious clothes with the emphasis on couture looks and fine jewelry. Other spectaculars may cover a specific market or a broad range.

The models can be society women, if it is a charity show. If the show is to be choreographed, models should be chosen first for their ability to move and second for their looks. Actors, actresses and dancers are excellent models. The choreographer can teach them routines quickly, which will cut down on rehearsal time—and expenses.

Music can be live or taped. If the budget permits, a composer can be hired to write a theme song or the music for the whole show. Live music creates a better impression and the musicians can usually pick up on the audience's mood. Taped music can be used as well—it can be taped for the show or selected from a library. Taped segments should be carefully coordinated to the total presentation and extra music added to each segment. This way, it can be edited or extended if the show is running faster or more slowly than expected.

In choosing a site, the size of the room and its facilities should determine the final choice. Local codes and union regulations should be investigated thoroughly. You may find that a quantity of union personnel—unfamiliar with fashion shows—may "go with the territory" and this has to be budgeted. Or that your ingenious table decorations don't conform to the fire laws or the health codes. Also, check to be sure storage space is available, security is tight and the room will be available for rehearsals.

HOW TO PRODUCE A FASHION SHOW

The annual Milliken Show, the last of the great spectaculars, has a $1.5 million budget and involves over 500 people.

Film, Tape and Television Presentations | 14

Film has been associated with the fashion show almost from the latter's inception. The first semi-annual Fall and Winter Fashion Show under the auspices of the National Retail Dry Goods Association, July 24–August 2, 1913, was the first widespread use of a filmed fashion presentation by retailers. *The American Cloak and Suit Review* announced:

> "The styles featured in the Exposition will be reproduced on moving picture films, which can be secured by retail sources for display in their local theaters."

And later:

> ". . . . pads and pencils busy, it was ascertained that many merchants had decided to use the moving pictures of the Fall and Winter Fashion Show in their stores as a drawing card at the Fall opening and had decided to purchase the very garments (that were filmed)."

The following year, at the Chicago Fall and Winter Style Show, the dress rehearsal was filmed—seven thousand feet of film was shot, covering nine scenes, for distribution to retailers.

Paul Poiret, on his first trip to the United States in 1913, brought a film of his clothes to show. Unfortunately it was considered so shocking—many of his gowns were slit to show boots or an occasional ankle—that the film was banned.

The first "mixed media" show was presented at the Chicago Trade Show in 1917, where filmed scenes were used to lead into each segment of the runway show.

Both film and slides began to be used extensively in the early Sixties giving the fashion show greater impact and immediacy. Most of the films produced around this time were done by fiber companies—primarily because of the cost. Norma Geer, fashion director of Celanese Fibers Company, was responsible for the development of two films to promote fibers to retailers and consumers. "Star in Crepe" was an extravaganza produced by Columbia Pictures with designs by

Paul Poiret's use of film was typical of his ability to adapt avant-garde techniques to fashion promotion. (KEYSTONE)

HOW TO PRODUCE A FASHION SHOW

Edith Head. "Fantasy in Fortrel," although the means of changing scenes were somewhat self-conscious by today's standards, was one of the earliest attempts to created an environment for the clothes shown. Both films enjoyed a successful run at stores around the country.

In 1966, director William Claxton and his wife and model, Peggy Moffitt, developed a film to demonstrate how entertaining high fashion on film could be. Titled "Basic Black," Rudi Gernreich's clothes were used to carry out the avant-garde theme. This same team was also involved in another Celanese effort, "Man in the Trevira Era," used as part of the introduction of that fiber in the United States in 1968.

Fashion shows were also being produced on television during this period. For several years during the early Sixties, some of the television networks produced a major show from Paris. In July, 1962, the networks got together (briefly) to stage a Telstar broadcast of some of the Paris Couture openings—specifically, Dior and Balenciaga. The furor was thunderous, but consumer reaction was drowned out by the industry in-fighting. While Dior and Balenciaga received enormous exposure and publicity, other members of the Chambre Syndicale, whose main function was to protect the couture against piracy, were furious. Some were envious, others were concerned that the telecast scooped press release dates. Meanwhile on Seventh Avenue, the big question was whether or not the higher priced segment of the market, which brought back styles from Europe to reproduce, would be undercut by the volume firms who might knock off the directional styles directly from the telecast. Which in turn could affect the retail promotions of the line-for-line copies. And as to the print media and their time schedules, *Women's Wear Daily* reported, somewhat self-servingly:

> "Slick fashion magazines—shackled to long lead times for mechanical reasons—will be among the first to suffer. The release date is their body armor to protect them from a faster moving daily newspaper competition.
>
> "The magazines now face a real drubbing editorially. Will their advertising linage suffer too? It's up to every advertiser now to decide whether to buy space in issues that may be lovely to look at but decidedly old for news."

During the latter part of the Sixties particularly, the Fashion Group produced some notable shows using both film and slides, sometimes both, to enhance their runway presentations. Rear screen projections were used, often with three or more screens employed simultaneously or at timed intervals.

Today, a network fashion show is still fairly uncommon. The "Today Show" carried the 1962 Telstar broadcast and continues to feature fashions from time to time. Local women's shows feature clothes on a more regular basis, particularly short seasonal presentations excerpted from a local retailer's seasonal show.

Film, Tape and Television—The Future

The number of fashion shows using film and/or slides as part of the staging should grow, since one of the hallmarks of the fashion show in the Seventies is

FILM, TAPE AND TELEVISION PRESENTATIONS

showing clothes in the context in which they'll be worn. This "environmental" presentation has proven effective over and over—the increased sales more than offsets the costs.

There are more end uses being developed for the show on film or tape. And this trend is being fueled by the heavier competition that retailers are facing. Many retailers tend to concentrate their resources on fewer, but larger live shows. These are interspersed with informal modeling and specialized presentations for small groups within a department.

Filmed and taped shows can be used as part of a large seasonal effort, in conjunction with a live show. In addition, they can be used between major promotional periods to create fashion excitement and they lend themselves to special interest markets.

Retailers are discovering that a major show can be taped and shown later in a department; it can be used as a sales training aid; copies can be sent to branches and portions can be lifted and used as television spots. On a prorated basis, the film becomes an efficient investment. In fact using filmed segments as television spots could put television advertising within the realm of more retailers, department stores particularly, than ever before.

Why Use Television?

The fashion industry, retailing in particular, has been traditionally print- rather than broadcast-oriented. While the largest percentage of chain and department store profits are coming from women's apparel, only a tiny percentage of their advertising budgets are devoted to advertising for this area, and the barest fraction of this to television. The major promotions tend to be primarily in national magazines and local newspapers. Local radio stations have been used fairly consistently, while television, until recently, has been used rarely and then only by chains and mass merchandisers promoting mostly hard goods. The resistance to television was based on the high costs of production and air time, the belief that more of their customers read newspapers, read them more consistently and spend more time with them. While television will never replace newspaper promotions —nor can certain types of merchandise be promoted profitably via television— there are large areas of merchandise and groups of retailers that can exploit television to a much greater advantage. And as the competition grows keener, retailers are taking a closer look at television.

Most stores face stiffer competition for consumer dollars because of pressing economic factors, changing consumer spending patterns and attitudes towards fashion (i.e., investment, more functional, multi-purpose clothes). The store must also contend with the expansion of drug, variety and mass merchandisers, even supermarkets, into what were traditional department store merchandise categories—and clientele.

Some stores will remain profitable by going the specialty store route and strengthening their appeal to a segmented market. Others will broaden their base, increasing their market area, going after new groups of potential customers, repositioning themselves more strongly to the current or occasional shopper.

Retailers looking to reach this larger audience would have to consider television as a part of the effort. Virtually every home has a television set and viewers spend an average of six hours a day in front of it. With this kind of an audience, a retailer can go a long way toward building awareness and decreasing threshold resistance —among people not being reached by print media.

Cost can be a serious factor, but not an insurmountable problem. A television spot alone can cost from an extreme low of $200 to a high of $25,000 to produce (more if re-shooting is necessary). On the other hand, a taped fashion show can cost between $2,000 and $4,000 a minute to film; several commercial spots can be lifted. (These are approximate costs. They will vary widely according to who produces and how elaborate the tape or spots are.)

Cost of air time varies widely from market to market and from one time period to another. Without ever going into prime time, however, an effective ad schedule can be set up that reaches prime prospects at a reasonable cost. Where the sales potential exists, cost should be weighed against increased sales volume—efficient use of dollars rather than increased expenditures. Furthermore, there are co-op dollars available from some vendors to defray expenses (which often go unspent, particularly by the smaller retail firms).

The Mechanics of Film and Tape

Filmed and taped fashion presentations are put together by independent producers, production studios or by working through agencies. (Many local television stations can recommend producers and advise on production and air time costs.) A television spot can take several days or several months to produce. The sponsoring film must discuss the concept with the producer in terms of audience, goals, budget, emphasis and time, among other things. It can take six weeks for a concept to be developed to the point where production can begin. The concept as it is presented by the producer most often includes a script, storyboard and cost estimate. The estimate will vary tremendously, based on the type and length of presentation, its elaborateness, the number of sets needed, production crew and model fees. When it is shot, the multi-purpose aspect is taken into consideration. Short segments, or "lift outs" or "take outs" can be taken out of fifteen to thirty minute shows to be used as commercials. "Take outs" of thirty or sixty second commercials can be removed for shorter spots. 8mm (rare), 16mm, 35mm and videotape can be used. The film is shot, edited and the picture and sound are mixed to produce the end product. The shooting to the final stage can take two and a half months. However, the "rushes" (footage shot in a single day) can be edited, put together with sound and completed in several days.

The In-House Studio

Many retailers are finding that there are so many uses for taped presentations, that it is more economical to establish their own studios to produce them. Saks

FILM, TAPE AND TELEVISION PRESENTATIONS

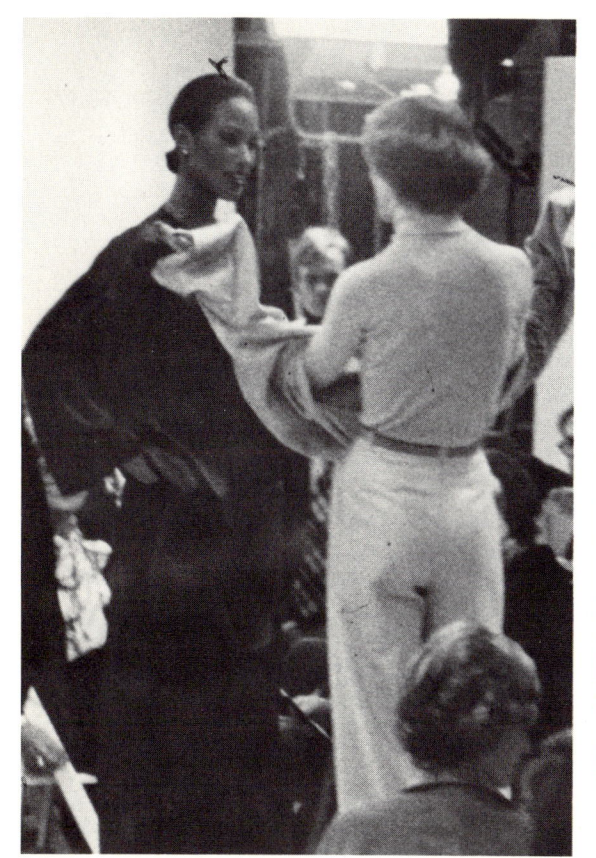

Above: Film is shot during presentation to key retailers. Above left: Models demonstrate layering techniques by swapping tops on runway.

Fifth Avenue (New York), while not the first to do this, is typical of the retailers with in-house studios that have sprung up recently. It does not produce commercial spots, but in the first year of operation it produced over fifty-six programs. The studio is an arm of the Training Department, headed by Beverly Cassidy, Corporate Director of Training and Development. Videotape Program Director Marsha Anderson runs the studio, organizing, taping, editing and dubbing each program.

Because stores are spread out geographically, the tapes (videotape is used exclusively) are part of a communication system that distributes the same information in exactly the same way to each store simultaneously. While the tapes are primarily used for the purpose of sales training, the studio has the capacity (with some adaptations) to film fashion shows for consumer viewing.

The content of the programs ranges from how to take inventory to how to wrap

HOW TO PRODUCE A FASHION SHOW

packages to interviews with major designers to coverage of new merchandise in various ready-to-wear categories.

On a yearly basis, a programming group decides the overall budget and what specific promotions and designers and topics will be produced. A schedule is made up that is flexible enough to accommodate changes during the year. Many of the buyers themselves will be responsible for organizing the programs on specific markets, while the studio will put together some of the others.

Most tapes run between ten and fifteen minutes. This is sufficient time to make the necessary points without losing the audience (they are presented at early morning staff meetings). Tapes being shown to customers within a department on a continuous basis can be much shorter.

The planning is a short version of a normal fashion show. The coordinator (buyer or merchandise manager) knows the approximate date of his tape in advance through the programming group. A week to ten days before shooting, he will be approached for a concept. He is also alerted to pull merchandise, accessories and props which can be stored in a small dressing room in the studio.

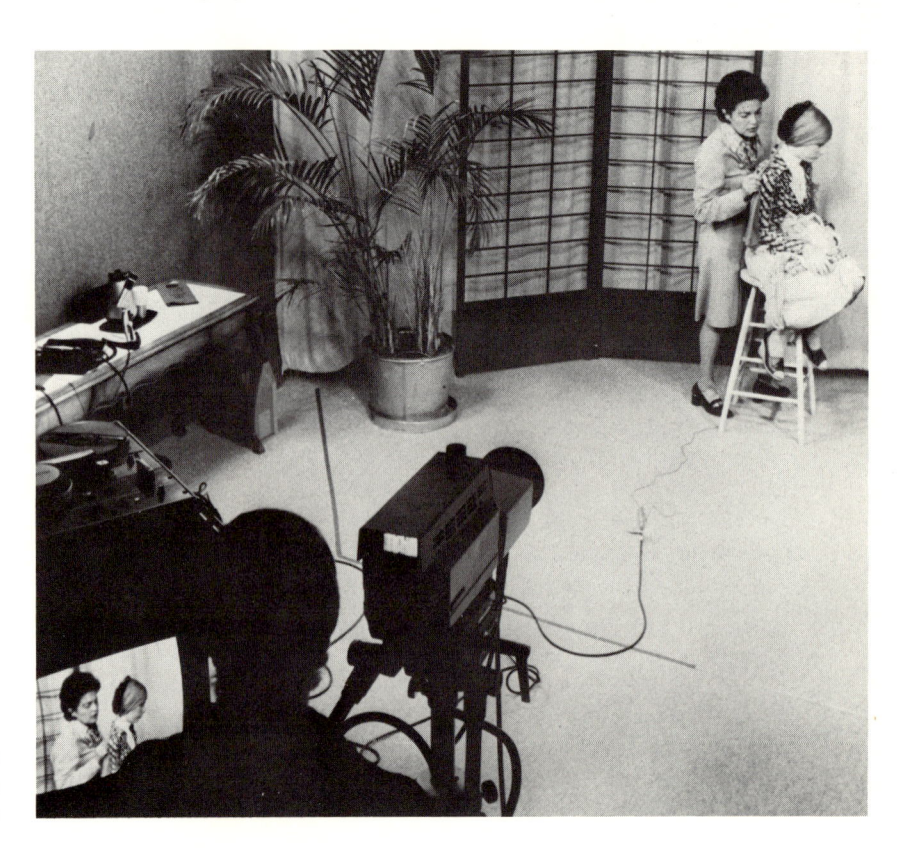

A buyer demonstrates head wrapping on her assistant for a sales training tape in Saks Fifth Avenue studio.

FILM, TAPE AND TELEVISION PRESENTATIONS

The display department will produce any signs needed and the models will be booked. Because it is easier to tape the complete presentation at one time (and substantially less costly if an outside studio is used), three or four models are booked for an hour.

Up to twenty-five pieces can be shown in fifteen minutes and a run-through is scheduled before the taping begins. The commentary may be delivered by the buyer or merchandise manager or it may be a conversation between a designer and the buyer. Cue cards are sometimes used, but the commentary is largely chatty and off-the-cuff. The sound is usually recorded at the same time (if a full-scale fashion show is being taped, the sound is usually recorded later—because the comments will become disjointed in the editing process).

After the presentation is taped, it may or may not be edited, and then it is screened for approval. The whole process of organizing, taping and editing averages about three hours per presentation.

Costs on setting up a studio will vary widely. The biggest expenditure will be for the construction of the studio itself with lighting, backdrop, dressing rooms and soundproofing as well as for the equipment to record and dub the programs. In addition, cassette players will be needed. Out-of-pocket costs on each program are kept to a minimum—sometimes co-oped with vendors. Programs at Saks averaged several hundred dollars each in their first year. Obviously, the cost per program will drop substantially over the subsequent years of operation without heavy start-up costs.

Sales Training Manual on new fashion looks accompanies Vogue *Magazine's New York Collection films.*

The Taped Fashion Show

Vogue Magazine's 16mm film of their annual New York fall retail fashion show based on the New York Collections is a good example of the show which is filmed simultaneously with the presentation. The concept is based on the merchandise representing key fall looks, and is planned and organized by the fashion department. Because the fashion show is geared to retail management, a broader, more conceptual approach is taken. The edited film will also be used by retailers for consumer and sales training presentations and for large charity events.

The format of the show is planned with a director, and an independent studio handles the production. The concept is developed in advance as key looks come out of market weeks, and is a continuation of early trends. Sixty garments are shown representing the major ready-to-wear categories, and the fashion points are emphasized.

During the show, several cameras are filming (16mm is used, which can be duplicated later or transferred to tape). Later the film is edited to approximately thirteen minutes. A script is written and the voiceover and music are added. *Vogue's* merchandising department also produces a sales training brochure for retailers in conjunction with the film, showing the fashion philosophy behind each major look, that acts as a guide to the salespeople to help them sell the clothes.

Bibliography

BOOKS

A History of Feminine Fashion (London and Cheltenham: Ed J. Burrow, 1927).

Bonney, Therese and Bonney, Louise. *A Shopper's Guide to Paris* (New York: Robert M. McBride, 1929).

Cassin-Scott, Jack. *Making Historical Costume Dolls* (London and Sydney: B.T. Botsford, 1975).

Chase, Edna Woolman and Chase, Ilka. *Always In Vogue* (New York: Doubleday, 1954).

Corinth, Kay. *Fashion Showmanship* (New York: John Wiley, 1970).

Crawford, M.D.C. *The Ways of Fashion* (New York: Fairchild Publications, Inc., 1948).

Curtis, Frieda Steinmann. *How To Give A Fashion Show* (New York: Fairchild Publications, Inc., 1950).

Davidson, William R. and Brown, Paul L. *Retailing Management* (New York: Ronald Press, 1960).

Fraser, Antonia. *Dolls* (London: Octopus Books, 1973).

Hawes, Elizabeth. *Fashion Is Spinach* (New York: Random House, 1938).

Jarrow, Jeanette A. and Judille, Beatrice. *Inside the Fashion Business* (New York: John Wiley, 1965).

Kotler, Philip. *Marketing Management: An Analysis, Planning, and Control* (Englewood Cliffs: Prentice-Hall, 1976).

Levin, Phyllis Lee. *The Wheels of Fashion* (Garden City: Doubleday, 1965).

Lewis, Mary E., in collaboration with Dignam, Dorothy. *The Marriage of Diamonds and Dolls* (New York: H.L. Lindquist, 1947).

Marcus, Stanley. *Minding The Store* (Boston: Little, Brown, 1974).

Pickens, Mary Brooks and Miller, Dora Loues. *Dressmakers of France* (New York: Harper & Row, 1956).

Saunders, Edith. *The Age of Worth* (Bloomington: Indiana University Press, 1955).

Singleton, Esther. *Dolls* (New York: Payson & Clark, 1927).

Starr, Laura B. *The Doll Book* (New York: Outing Publishing, 1908).

PERIODICALS

The American Cloak and Suit Review. Issues of May, June, July, August, September, October, 1913; April 1914.

"The Dressmakers of France," *Fortune*, August 1932.

"He Was Once a King of Fashion," *St. Louis Post-Dispatch*, November 3, 1935.

The New York Times, May 3, 1944.

"Organization and Background of the Couture —Ornament to World Civilization," Barbas, Raymond, *Paris Today*, September 1951.

"Poiret the Magnificent Grasshopper," Morrill, Lowell, *The American Weekly*, June 18, 1944.

"TVB Stages How-To for Putting Co-Op $ To Work," Christopher, Maurine, *Advertising Age*, October 13, 1975.

Vogue Magazine, The Condé Nast Publications, Inc., February 1974.

Women's Wear Daily, Fairchild Publications, Inc. Issues of August 10, 11, 1910; September 19, 20, 1911; March 19, 1912; August 10, 1912; July 25, 26, 1962; August 8, 21, 1962; October 16, 1973; November 27, 28, 29, 1973; December 18, 1973.

Index

accessories, 46-47, 48
advertising, 109-113
   bridal show, 119
   budget, 113
   home sewing show, 122
   newspaper, 111-12
   radio, 112-13
   size and frequency, 110-11
   teen show, 123
   television, 113
American Cloak and Suit Review, The, 7-8, 137
Anderson, Marsha, 141
Anne, Queen of Brittany, 1
audience, 27-33

backdrop, 89
   bridal show, 119
   children's show, 125
   home sewing show, 122
   teen show, 123
Balenciaga, 138
bandbox show, 25, 126-27
"Basic Black," 138
Bertin, Rose, 2, 5
bridal show, 9, 23, 117-19

Cassidy, Beverly, 141
Celanese Fibers Company, 137, 138
Chambre Syndicale, 138
charity show, 23, 127
Charles VI, King of France, 1
Chase, Edna Woolman, 8

Chicago Century of Progress Exhibition, 1933-34, 10
Chicago Fall and Winter Style Show, 1914, 8, 137
Chicago Trade Show, 1917, 137
children's show, 124-25
   models, 61, 124-25
Claxton, Peggy Moffitt, 138
Claxton, William, 138
college show, 123-24
color, 43
commentary, 78-82. *See also* commentator
   ad-libs, 79-80
   children's show, 125
   co-commentary, 80-81
   home sewing show, 121-22
   mature woman's show, 125
   show without, 82
   taped show, 143
   teen show, 123
   trade show, 132-133
   types of, 79-81
   writing, 81
commentary cards, 51
commentator, 71-78. *See also* commentary
   arrangements with, 77-78
   bridal show, 119
   celebrities and personalities, 77-78
   fashion coordinator, 76
   free-lance commentator, 76
   home sewing show, 122
   magazine commentator, 76
   manufacturer's representative, 76-77

INDEX

presentation, 72
qualifications, 71-72
teen show, 123
trade show, 132
types of, 75-77
co-op show, 23, 126, 127
Coty American Fashion Critics Award, 11
courriers, 1
Couture Group, 11
crinoline, 5

Deering Milliken Breakfast Show, 11, 12, 66, 132, 133, 136
designer show, 23, 127-28, 131
Dior, 138
displays, 90, 97-98
  in-store displays, 97-98
  timing, 98
  window displays, 97
dolls. *See* model dolls
Doucet, 6
dramatized show, 23, 25
dress rehearsal, 55, 57
dressers, 88
  bridal show, 119
Dufy, Raoul, 6

Erté, 6
Eugénie, Empress of France, 5

"Fantasy in Fortrel," 138
fashion babies, 1
fashion coordinator, 76
fashion dolls. *See* model dolls
"Fashion Futures," New York, 1935, 10-11
Fashion Group, 10-11
fashion models. *See* models
fashion parade, 21-22
  types of, 23
fashion show. *See also* specific topics
  background planning, 27-40
  evaluation, 18-19
  history, 1-12
  location, 33-34

merchandise planning, 41-48
packing up, 57-58
  personnel, 88-89
  purpose, 13-19
  theme, 43-44
  timing, 34-37, 45
  types of, 21-26
film presentation, 137-43
finale, 53-54
Fitting Room Check List, 50
fitting sheets, 50, 51
fittings, 49-50
floor plan, 83-90
  entrances and exits, 86-87
  model room, 87-88
  runway. *See* runway
  stage, 83-84

Gagelin & Opigez, 5
garment tags, 50-51, 53
Geer, Norma, 137
Gernreich, Rudi, 138
girdle, 6
giveaways, 95
  bridal show, 119
  home sewing show, 122
  teen show, 123
  trade show, 133

hatbox show, 25, 126-27
hobble skirt, 6
home sewing show, 25, 120-22
Hotel Rambouillet, Paris, 1
House of Paquin, etc. *See* Paquin, House of, etc.
how to show, 25

Ideal Chart, 44, 45-46, 47, 50
informal show, 25-26
  models, 62
inventory sheets, 48
invitations, 91-94
  bridal show, 119
  distribution, 93-94
  home sewing show, 122

INDEX

teen show, 123
trade show, 133
types of, 92-93
Iribe, Paul, 6
Isabella, Queen of Bavaria, 1
Isabella, Queen of Spain, 1

Lambert, Eleanor, 11
Legros, 2
Lepape, Georges, 6
lighting, 90
little ladies, 1

magazine commentators, 76
magazines
    promotional tie-ins, 101-4, 105, 106
male models, 8, 62
"Man in the Trevira Era," 138
mannequins, 5
manufacturer tie-ins, 104-5, 107
manufacturer's representatives, 76-77
March of Dimes fashion show, 11, 129
Marcus, Herbert, 9
Marcus, Stanley, 9
Marie Antoinette, 2
market area, 28, 30-31
marketing, 13-14
mature woman's show, 125-26
    models, 61, 125
Medici, Maria de, 1-2
Merchandise Buyers Exposition and Fashion Show, New York, 1912, 7
merchandise planning, 41-48
    accessories, 46-47, 48
    grouping, 52
    hang tags and cards, 48
    Ideal Chart, 44, 45-46, 47, 50
    inventory sheets, 48
    shoes, 48
merchandising, 13-14
Milliken Breakfast Show. *See* Deering Milliken Breakfast Show
model dolls, 1-7
model room, 87-88
model sheets, 50, 51, 54-55

models, 59-60
    amateur, 60-61
    booking, 64, 66
    bridal show, 118-19
    children's show, 61, 124-25
    evaluation, 66
    fees, 66-67
    gifts, 66-67
    home sewing show, 121
    informal, 62
    male, 8, 62
    mature woman's show, 61, 128
    professional, 60-61
    professional standards, 62-63
    qualifications, 59-60
    size, 59
    society women, 61
    sources, 64, 65
    spectacular, 135
    teen show, 61, 123
    trade show, 132
    training, 67-69
Moffitt, Peggy, 138
movie studios, use of fashion show by, 10
music, 9, 90

National Retail Dry Goods Association, 137
Neiman-Marcus, 9
New York Times, The
    "Fashions of the Times," 11
newspapers
    advertising, 111-12
    promotional tie-ins, 118
    older woman's show. *See* mature woman's show

pandoras, 1, 2,
Paquin, House of, 6, 7
parade. *See* fashion parade
Patou, Jean, 6
Poiret, Paul, 5-6, 7, 8, 137
poupées, 1
press kits, 116
press releases, 114, 116

INDEX

pressers, 88
prizes, 99-101
profit, 19
programs, 95-97
promotion, 15, 31, 91-98
   displays. *See* displays
   prizes, 99
   tie-ins. *See* tie-ins
props, 89
publicity, 113-16
   photos and captions, 116
   press releases, 114
   sources, 114
   trade show, 133
puppets, 1

Quant, Mary, 12, 82

radio
   advertising, 112-13
   presentation, 10
   promotional tie-ins, 108
Ray, Man, 6
Rayograph, 6
ready-to-wear, 7, 9
Réjane, 6
refreshments, 90
Responsibility Sheet, 38, 39-40
retailing, 13-16
run-off, 51-53, 54
   bridal show, 118
   home sewing show, 121
   trade show, 130-32
run-through, 55, 57
runway, 7, 21-22, 84-85
   T-shaped, 84
   Y-shaped, 84

Saks Fifth Avenue, New York, 140-41, 143
Sanger Bros., 9
school show, 124
sewing show. *See* home sewing show
Shenk Store, Lebanon, Pa., 7-8
shoes, 48

specialty shows, 23
spectacular, 11, 25, 133, 135-36
   fashion parade, 53
sports clothes, 6
staging, 89
   bridal show, 119
   home sewing show, 122
   teen show, 123
"Star in Crepe," 137-38
starters, 88
   children's show, 125
Steichen, Edward, 6
style show, 16
stylists, 88

Teatts, Hannah, 2
teen show, 122-23
   models, 61, 123
television
   advertising, 113
   presentation, 139-40
   promotional tie-ins, 108
tickets, 94-95
tie-ins, 99-108
   bridal show, 119
   home sewing show, 122
   teen show, 123
Tobé, 10
"Today" show, 138
trade show, 7, 23, 129-30, 132-33
trunk show, 23, 128

Vernet, Marie, 5
Vogue
   Fashion Fête, 5, 8-9
   filmed shows, 143
   Model Doll Show, 2-4

Wanamaker, John, 8
window displays, 97
Women's Wear Daily (formerly *Women's Wear*), 7, 138
Worth, Charles Frederick, 5
Worth, House of, 5, 6
Worth, Marie Vernet, 5